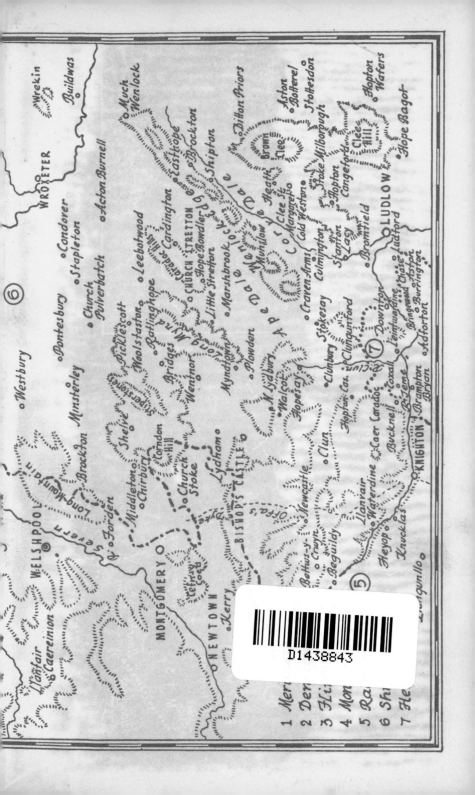

1 LLANTHONY PRIORY, MONMOUTHSHIRE

*From a Water-Colour
by J. M. W. Turner*

THE FACE OF BRITAIN

WELSH BORDER COUNTRY

By

P. THORESBY JONES, M.A.

SOMETIME SCHOLAR OF CHRIST CHURCH, OXFORD

*Illustrated from Photographs and
Sketches*

LONDON
B. T. BATSFORD LTD.
15 NORTH AUDLEY STREET, W.1

First Published, April 1938

MADE AND PRINTED IN GREAT BRITAIN
FOR THE PUBLISHERS, B. T. BATSFORD LTD., LONDON
BY MORRISON AND GIBB LTD., TANFIELD, EDINBURGH

PREFACE

WHEN I was asked by the publishers to contribute a volume on the Welsh Border to form the sixth volume of "The Face of Britain" Series, I undertook the commission with considerable pleasure, because I have always felt that this particular tract of country, as remarkable for the impressive beauty of its landscape as for its romantic past and its historic buildings, has never been appreciated or visited by the majority of English people, who are frequently curiously ignorant of some of the finest phases of their many-sided inheritance.

I had already contributed a small volume on this area to a little series issued by the British Publishing Co., Gloucester, and I can at least claim that this volume is the result of first-hand experience extending over a great number of years, for, practically without exception, I have myself personally traced out the routes given and have visited the scenes and buildings described. In order to allow even a fairly slender treatment, it has been necessary to limit myself to a comparatively compact strip of country on both sides of the actual topographical Border. I have not confined myself to the English side, for the wavering Border marks no logical division, and it is necessary, in order to understand the countryside, to cross it in both directions. Naturally, it has been found impracticable to attempt to treat, even in the most cursory way, of the whole of the ten counties through which the Border passes. I have sought to deal more extensively with the more out-of-the-way and less-known places, such as the Black Mountains, which even yet are comparatively little known or visited. On the other hand, even making the fullest use of the text space at my disposal in the Series, it has been necessary to condense most rigorously the text which I had written, and I hope, therefore, that lovers of this country who find that their favourite spots are cursorily dismissed or passed without mention will realize that it is a case of necessity and not of choice.

The neglect of the district is shown in the comparative difficulty of obtaining a good series of illustrations of its landscapes, especially of the more remote districts. Justice has not been done pictorially to the beauty of its countryside beyond a

few well-known spots. It was feared that it would be a troublesome or impossible task to obtain a really representative series
of pictures, but I am pleased to think that the special measures
adopted by the publishers have been crowned with success,
and that within the limits a really fine and varied series of
typical photographs has been assembled. If this series of
pictures, together with the accompanying text, results in my
favourite country being better known and appreciated and
more thoroughly visited, I shall be amply repaid for the years
during which I have wandered over it and the labour that I
have devoted to the compilation of this work.

P. THORESBY JONES.

LONDON, *February* 1938.

ACKNOWLEDGMENT

THE Publishers must acknowledge their obligation to the photographers whose work is reproduced in these pages, namely: Mr. Antony Brown, for Fig. 105; Mr. W. A. Call, for Fig. 40; the late Brian C. Clayton, for Figs. 13, 27–32, 41, 42, 44, 58, 59, 62, 63, 98, 124–126; Mr. J. Dixon-Scott, F.R.P.S., for Figs. 8, 16, 17, 21, 22, 23, 38, 39, 43, 48, 53, 55, 93, 94, 101, 122; Mr. Herbert Felton, F.R.P.S., for Figs. 6, 78, 81, 82, 91, 95, 99, 115, 118; Messrs. Fox Photos, for Figs. 7, 109, 120, 121; Mr. E. Chambré Hardman, F.R.P.S., for Figs. 88, 107, 112 ; Miss Joan Parry, for Figs. 9, 45, 50, 52; Mr. H. Stubington, for Figs. 2–4, 11, 14, 15, 19, 20, 25, 33, 36, 37, 54, 66, 68, 69, 71, 77, 87, 92, 97, 100, 102, 103, 104, 106, 108, 111, 113, 114; *The Times*, for Figs. 5, 80; Mr. Will F. Taylor, for Figs. 10, 18, 26, 34, 35, 46, 47, 51, 56, 61, 67, 72–74, 76, 83–85, 89, 96, 110, 116, 117, 119, 123, 127–129; Mr. H. S. L. Watkins, for Fig. 86; Mr. W. J. H. Watkins, for Figs. 49, 70, 75, 79; Miss M. Wight, for Figs. 57, 64, 65. The Frontispiece has been reproduced from the original water-colour by kind permission of the owner, Mr. Walter Stoye.

In view of the out-of-the-way character of the district, and the frequent difficulty of obtaining clearly defined photographic results on account of a frequent subtle diffused haze, the publishers must express their appreciation of the co-operation of a number of photographers who have made special efforts and taken several journeys over the area. They are especially grateful to Mr. W. F. Taylor, Mr. Herbert Felton, and Mr. H. Stubington, who, having the advantage of residing on the ground, has been unwearied in making numerous trips all over the Border country and taking a large number of views, from which the present representative selection has been made. The tailpieces by Mr. Sydney R. Jones are from works illustrated by him and issued by the publishers, and those by the late H. T. Timmins are from his twin volumes on *Nooks and Corners in Shropshire* and *Herefordshire*. The map endpapers have been specially prepared by Miss Norah Davenport.

CONTENTS

2 VALE AND HILL: VIEW TOWARDS PRESTEIGN AND KNILL, FROM BYTON, WAPLEY HILL ON LEFT

b

3 CLOUD OVER THE BLACK MOUNTAINS: NORTHERN
ESCARPMENT AT RHOS DIRION

WELSH BORDER COUNTRY

CHAPTER I

GENERAL INTRODUCTION: THE LORDS MARCHERS: PEOPLES OF THE WELSH BORDERLAND: SOME APOLOGIES: MODES OF TRANSPORT

WANDERING to and fro across the arbitrary border-line between England and Wales those wayfarers-by-choice who delight in fine scenery will find a rich banquet of diversified courses spread before their eyes, and a pervading charm that must satisfy the most fastidious of æsthetic cravings. Of spectacular scenery there is little, though a first view of the Breiddens is startling, and the escarpments of the Black Mountains and their neighbours the Beacons range from the impressive to the fantastic; while there are lines and groups of hills, like the Clwydians and the heights about Church Stretton, on which gradients and outlines confer the dignity of mountains. What the Welsh Border may be said to specialize in is a blend of opulence and wildness; the typical prospect is a richly timbered valley with a high moorland background.

Lowland scenery puts on its richest dress—pasture and arable in tree-fringed fields often interrupted by tree-mantled isolated hills—where the "plain-tracks" of Wye and Usk skirt the western moors of Herefordshire and Monmouthshire, and again in Shropshire, where the rivers break away from the uplands. Along the western side of the Border is a succession of rolling multi-coloured moorlands stretching from the widespread, lofty Berwyns to the still loftier Black Mountains, with their oft-repeated alternation of heathery ridge and delightful valley; between these lie Clun Forest and Kerry Hill, and the bulky Radnor Forest with its wonderful Harley Valley. These moorlands are pranked with bright-green valleys marking the upper courses of a score of rivers: Ceiriog, Vyrnwy, Tanat, Onny, Teme, Lugg, Arrow and

Honddu, Monnow and Grwyne Fawr, and, most exquisite of all, Grwyne Fechan. Larger-scale valley scenery reaches perfection in the Vale of Clwyd, gorge scenery in the Vale of Llangollen. West of Ludlow a welter of hills and miniature ravines, centring on The Goggin and the labyrinthine Deerfold Forest, will repay rambling in any detail. If you are one of those enlightened few—either fools or philosophers the multitude deems them—who derive a strangely thrilling pleasure from ridge-walking in solitude, here are the long Shropshire hog's-backs and, once again, the Black Mountains with fifty miles of ridges untenanted save by sheep, hill ponies, grouse and wilder birds.

To sum up, the great appeal of this hilly countryside is in its blending of the rich grace of the English landscape with the impressive dignity of real, even if miniature, mountains, to be found only in a smaller area, if on an intenser scale, in the Lake District. It is not, like the North and South-West, a moorland mass or plateau dissected by river valleys; it is rather an undulating plain broken by tangled or straight hill-ridges, often densely forested. Its wildflowers are abundant, its autumn colouring glorious, but for the view-collector the district is without a parallel—prospects of delight unfold themselves from most hilltops or ridge-edges, and, as the very representative illustrations testify, each has its distinctiveness in spite of a strong cousinly likeness. But finally I would put in a strong claim for the hundreds of miles of the hill lanes of the Border; often a riot of wildflowers, ferns and bushes, winding beneath hilly high banks, or shading into moorland tracks, they put the rambler on intimate terms with the countryside, its human life, fauna and flora. My remembrances of the joys of their exploration is tinged with the regret that there are so many of necessity left unexplored or not revisited.

Then all along the Border you shall find in profusion works of man that detain the curious and evoke ejaculations even from the Philistine. Prehistoric "camps"; early Norman mottes; ancient castles, abbeys and churches; Tudor and Jacobean manor-houses, farm-dwellings and cottages—here you shall encounter all these in a variety and condition to delight not only the antiquarian but the artist and the amateur of beauty in stone, brick and timber. Timber above all, for this is the country of the "black and white," the country where John Abel flourished and where timber-framing reached its zenith. Here are fascinating villages and little towns—Eardisland and Yarpole, Weobley and Pembridge—built

4 THE NORTHERN BORDER: THE VALE OF CLWYD, WITH MOEL FAMMAU IN THE MIDDLE OF THE RIDGE

5 THE SEVERN COUNTRY: MONTGOMERY CASTLE AND THE LONG MOUNTAIN, FROM TOWN HILL

wholly in this style. Mention of buildings reminds me of
something that is of paramount importance to all who take
the road: in this sequestered Borderland the discerning
traveller can still find plenty of old-fashioned—not *too* old-
fashioned—inns of the kind that sportsmen use; inns that
provide not frigid luxury but warm comfort and personal
service, and beatify the toils of a topographical day with a
termination restful and agreeable.

Of the larger Border towns, Shrewsbury and Hereford,
Ludlow and Leominster both enthral the sightseer and give
the lover of history ample material for rumination. As for
that, the whole Borderland, for centuries the tilting-ground
of well-matched races and factions, is a rich storehouse of
moving incidents and of names that made history; nor does
this region need the artificial enhancement of book-made
romance; for this was the land of the Lords Marchers, of de
Braoses and de Bohuns, of Fulk Fitzwarine and Geoffrey of
Monmouth, perhaps of Arthur and Gwenhwyfar—a very
home of romance.

Any detailed topographical account of the Welsh Border
must necessarily contain frequent references to the Lords
Marchers, and must therefore pluck a few strands from the
intricately tangled skein of Border history: must at least try
briefly to explain why the Marcher-Lordship system was
established, how it worked, where the chief lordships were
and what families ruled them at salient periods. The Anglo-
Saxons had rarely penetrated into and still more rarely settled
in any part of what is now Wales: Offa's Dyke marks pretty
accurately the western limit of their power. William I's
initial success at Battle was promptly followed up, and
within a few years he had gained complete military ascendancy
over the English of the English plain. He was well aware
that beyond the western confines of what had been Mercia
lay a country of intricate difficulty peopled by no "tame
villatic fowl" but guarded by fierce warriors trained in constant fighting; at the same time it was now urgently necessary
that he should plan the administration and survey the re-
sources of his new English kingdom; and many of his "Com-
panions," more adapted to camps than to council-chambers,
were likely to get in the way or even cause active annoyance
unless given tasks that both engrossed and satisfied them.
His ingenuity solved the difficulty: selecting those of his
knights who were apt to be insubordinate he bade each of them
conquer a bit of Wales for himself, with the promise that what

any of them gained from the Welsh he should rule as a miniature kingdom.

Thus came into being the Lords Marchers, so-called because they carved out lordships in a region that became the *march* (mark: dividing-line) between the English kingdom and the country ruled by Welsh princes. It was not till near the end of Rufus's reign that the majority of the marcher lordships took definite shape; and down to 1284, when Edward I annexed the dominions of the Welsh princes, the border-line between the native principality and the March was never a fixed boundary; under stress of the valiant resistance periodically offered by the Welsh under such princely leaders as Owen Gwynedd, Llewelyn ap Iorwerth (Llewelyn the Great) and Llewelyn ap Gruffydd, it was a line ever advancing and receding and at times fluctuating violently.

Certain of the greater lordships marcher became palatine earldoms before William I's death—Chester under Hugh of Avranches, Shrewsbury under Roger of Montgomery,[1] Hereford under William FitzOsborn. Later, there was a royal palatinate of Cheshire, and the greater portions of what are now Shropshire and Herefordshire were made counties, though from these English counties and one or two others as well as from four of the six Welsh counties formed by Edward I, certain districts that now belong to them were excluded as being marcher lordships. Other great marcher lordships that received the organization (but not the status) of counties were Pembrokeshire and the Vale of Glamorgan.

A knight who was chartered to gain a marcher lordship for himself would, after selecting his objective, start operations by constructing at some strategic point a motte and bailey— a mound strengthened by palisade and ditch and adjoined by a court with an earthwork rampart likewise palisaded and moated. When the inhabitants of the selected district had been subdued, he or a successor built a stone castle, and about it a little town, to which English and Norman settlers were invited, and which later became a market and trading centre: it also comprised a special Welsh quarte. One often finds the original motte-and-bailey surmounted by or, as at Clifford and Longtown, a mile or two distant from the ruins of the later masonry castle.

Not all the marcher lordships were founded by force of arms; a few were actually bestowed on Brythonic chieftains, and sometimes the Norman free-lance married the daughter

[1] See pp. 6 and 93.

6 LUDLOW CASTLE AND DINHAM BRIDGE OVER THE TEME

7 THE UPPER WYE IN PERHAPS ITS MOST BEAUTIFUL STRETCH, BETWEEN BUILTH AND RHAYADER

8   THE LOWER WYE: THE FAMOUS VIEW AT SYMOND'S YAT, BETWEEN HUNTSHAM HILL AND COPPIT HILL

9 "BLACK AND WHITE": THE OLD MARKET HALL AND NEW
INN, PEMBRIDGE

of a chieftain and acquired a lordship by inheritance. No racial or social inhibition stood in the way of such marriages: later we find Llewelyn ap Iorwerth wedded to a natural daughter of King John, and a Mortimer to Llewelyn's daughter; and all Glyndwr's daughters had English husbands of knightly rank. This raises an important point. According to one very reasonable anthropological theory, the Neolithic inhabitants of Britain—short, dark, vivacious, a pastoral people skilful with their hands but with no knowledge of the use of iron— were the ancestors of the general substratum of the Welsh people[1]: some scientists call them the "Iberian" stock. Long before Cæsar's time, Celtic invaders crossed the narrow seas in two successive migrations: first came the Goidels, who left little impression on South or West Britain[2] but were driven across to Ireland or up to the Scottish highlands by the second horde, the Brythons, who knew the use of iron. The Brythons were tall, blonde and blue-eyed, not unlike Teutons: they overran and settled extensively in the lowland parts of the country and imposed their language—from which modern Welsh is descended—on all Britain south of the Clyde and the Cheviots; they did not penetrate into Wales *en masse*, but became the dominant caste there: the Welsh princely houses were of Brythonic, not "Iberian" stock, whence it comes that Welsh poets when they indite compliments to the wives and daughters of their aristocratic Welsh patrons dwell upon their golden tresses, caerulean eyes, dazzlingly fair complexions and white arms and bosoms. Such physical traits are not un- common to-day along the Wye and Severn valleys, where anthropologists say the Brythonic mass-invasion halted.

This theory should not seem paradoxical. The Brythonic and Anglo-Saxon invaders were not accompanied by many of their own women, and in those days women were among the first-fruits of victory—"to every man a damsel or two"—and were annexed, not slaughtered; the Brython or Saxon warrior carried off any "Iberian" woman that took his fancy, and of children born of the resulting unions a fair proportion sur- vived: cross-breeds are tough. Scientists again come forward to tell us that the "Iberian" stock has far more "genetic per- sistency" than blond stocks; and that in our larger English

[1] And, to a certain extent, of the population-substratum of the western half of the England.

[2] Except for two "enclaves" of Goidels, in historical times known as the "red-haired banditti of Dinas Mawddwy" and the "Plant Matt" (Martha's pro- geny), and shunned like lepers by the rest of the population. Both gangs were exterminated in Elizabeth's reign.

towns, as a result of urbanization, there is a constant and pro-
gressive diminution of blond types and a corresponding
increase of the "Iberian." Nor must we forget that the whole
of Great Britain is populated by mongrels. If on one side of
the Border we have

"That heterogeneous thing, an Englishman,"

the Welshman on the other side is even more heterogeneous;
and along the Border racial intermixture was intensified.

We have seen that marriages between Norman and Brython
were not looked on as *mésalliances*. But when a Saxon or
Norman lord, as sometimes happened, became sufficiently
enamoured of a Cymric woman to marry her, the fact was
shrouded in a mist of magic and miracle—a concession to a
kind of snobbery. The bride, always small and a brunette, is
a fairy, an elfin creature who will disappear if allusion is made
to her origin; or she "comes from the hills," and if she touches
iron some disaster will result (the "Iberians" did not use iron).
One legend of Wild Eadric, Saxon Earl of Shrewsbury, illus-
trates this point well. Eadric constantly harassed his sup-
planter, Roger of Montgomery, but at last was persuaded by
Ralph Mortimer to swear allegiance to the Conqueror. Afterwards he wooed a fairy maiden of Clun Forest, who agreed
to wed him on condition that he should never afterwards
allude to her supernatural origin. The couple were married in
Westminster Abbey, the king himself being present; the
description in a contemporary Latin chronicle would well fit
a present-day fashionable wedding at St. Margaret's. The
mésalliance turned out quite successful for a time; both husband
and wife were happy, and a child was born to them; but one
day during a conjugal squabble Eadric forgot his promise
and made some nasty remark about his fairy sisters-in-law;
whereupon the well-loved form of his dark-eyed darling
became blurred and unsubstantial, and finally vanished in a
swirl of tenuous vapour; and the once happy warrior was left
literally holding the baby.

The marcher lordships with which the student of Border
topography should make himself acquainted formed a con-
tinuous string from north to south. I give, adding locations
where necessary, all but those of little importance: Rhuvoniog
(Denbigh and the Hiraethog), Kimmerch (south of Denbigh),
Dyffryn Clwyd (Ruthin district), Mold, Yale (Alun valley),
Bromfield (Wrexham and Ellesmere district), Chirk, Oswestry,
Whittington, Pool (Welshpool), Chirbury, Montgomery,

10 THE BERWYN MOORLANDS AT THE TOP OF THE MILLTIR
CERRIG PASS

11 RADNOR FOREST: IN THE HARLEY VALLEY

12 THE BRECON BEACONS FROM BRECON CASTLE

Powysland (part of Montgomeryshire[1]), Kerry, Cydowain (Newtown district), Clun, Wigmore, Maelynydd (N. Radnorshire[1]), Radnor, Elvael (S. Radnorshire[1]), Eardisley, Clifford, Ewyas (Llanthony and Longtown districts), Dinas (near Talgarth), Blaenllyfni (near Bwlch), Brecon with Hay, Abergavenny, Honour of Monmouth (Monmouth with the "Trilateral" (see p. 35)), Gwenllwg, Over Went, Nether Went: the last four together made up what is now Monmouthshire; the Wents apparently comprised some twenty-four minor lordships, some of which were sometimes held independently.

The system lasted till its abolition by Henry VIII; but gradually the killing-off of male stocks (the fighting lord seldom reached middle age), marriages of heiresses, escheatals and transferences concentrated the bulk of the lordships in comparatively few hands. Thus the de Lacy lordships came into possession of Edmund of Lancaster and, later, of the Crown in the person of Henry IV, who also by marrying Mary de Bohun acquired half the de Bohun estates (see below); the vast array of Mortimer lordships was inherited by Edward of York, afterwards Edward IV (see p. 54); and the Yorkist lordships were added to the Lancastrian when Henry VII was crowned.

Certain criticisms of Owen Glyndwr in this volume may give offence. They proceed, however, from a genuine belief that Owen Glyndwr, so far from meriting the title of Welsh patriot, did the Welsh people long-lasting damage, first by using Welsh soldiers wholesale as arrow-fodder, secondly by arousing in the English an exaggerated panic which resulted in the enactment of savage penal laws against the Welsh. Glyndwr, so far from feeling patriotic prejudices, was even in early manhood, when such prejudices are strongest, an Anglophil. Brought up partly at the English court, he married a Hanmer of Hanmer Hall in Maelor Saesneg (Saxon Maelor); and for his daughters' husbands he selected English county magnates—a Mortimer, a Scudamore, a Croft.[2] He was in his own eyes one of the English nobility; and when Grey de Ruthyn by a dirty act of treachery cheated him out of a manorial property, it was not so much the material loss that made him so bitterly revengeful as the loss of territorial title and the feeling that Grey had treated him as an inferior. Megalomania, the reverse side of the inferiority complex, showed itself later in a vaulting ambition bound to o'erleap itself: he and his English and Scotch allies—the Percies and

[1] *i.e.* what eventually was comprised in that shire.
[2] The Crofts prided themselves on their pure Anglo-Saxon descent.

Douglas—were to partition England between them; though when he made this compact he had lost the pick of his fighting-men and could recruit only youths. That he had this morbid streak in him seems highly probable: it explains the wild language and claims to magical power that Shakespeare put in his mouth, perhaps in accordance with a tradition; it explains also his sulky retirement after his final failure, and his unknightly refusal of a pardon proffered by a knightly foe.

To the antiquarian and the topographer Glyndwr's worst crime was his senseless, wholesale destruction of castles, abbeys, churches and manor-houses, even of whole towns; whether these were built or held by Englishmen or Welshmen made no difference to him. Architectural remains cannot be weighed against the welfare of a people; but so far from benefiting the Welsh, he denuded Wales of a generation of warriors and was responsible for the penal laws that crippled her for another generation. He did not "champion" the Welsh people: he used them. He could beat the patriotic drum with skill—but one of Dr. Johnson's definitions of *patriotism* seems to fit his case. A large number of influential, representa-tive Welshmen—politic, long-headed men who studied the true interests and material welfare of their fellow-countrymen —persistently opposed him from the start. Among them were William-ap-Thomas of Raglan, the "blue Knight of Gwent," progenitor of the famous Herberts, his father-in-law Dafydd Gam, and Vaughans of several branches.

It may be thought odd that in later pages I describe so much of the Mary Webb country without more than a casual allusion to Mary Webb's works. This is not an oversight. Before I had got through more than one of the Webb novels I read and hilariously reread Stella Gibbons' *Cold Comfort Farm*; and this cruelly clever, if tomboyish, parody of a type[1] has, for me at any rate, effectually "killed" all those stark, grim novels about the good red earth and so forth which, though they may win praise from overworked Prime Ministers, depict a rural life that happily is never met with outside their de-pressing pages. Miss Gibbons, like Cervantes, has pricked a balloon of literary humbug.

You cannot see this lovely Borderland satisfactorily from a car. A car will be useful for approaching the Borderland in comfort, or for quick transport to any particular place on the Border that you wish to examine at leisure—say Ludlow town

[1] The arch-exponent of this type is not Mary Webb, but Sheila Kaye-Smith.

13 THE VILLAGE OF RUARDEAN, ON THE EDGE OF THE FOREST OF DEAN, LOOKING TOWARDS
THE BLACK MOUNTAINS

14   THE WALL-LIKE EASTERN RIDGE OF THE BLACK MOUNTAINS, WITH BLACK HILL ON THE RIGHT

or White Castle or Abbey Dore church. But for appreciation of scenery or for topographical study of a countryside, motoring is far too rapid a mode of motion. Walking is the best method for the exploration of a limited area of great possibilities, such as the Black Mountains or Deerfold Forest or the head of the Vale of Clwyd; but you cannot cover the whole Border on foot unless you have unlimited leisure.

The despised push-bike offers a convenient compromise; but there are certain districts where tracks are so few and so difficult that to cover an adequate amount of space in the day it is necessary to combine walking and bicycling—to use a push-bike where you can, and *lug* or carry your bike where riding is impracticable or dangerous. I have thus been able to cross the three roughest and steepest Black Mountains passes and the Stiperstones, taking them in my stride, so to speak, as parts of circular day-tours. The Bwlch-y-Trumau and Grwyne Fechan round I have done thus several times without over-exertion; and I am far from young. For such definite purposes I can confidently recommend the ride-and-lug method.

In the next chapter I plunge *more Homerico* into the middle of my subject—or somewhere near the middle—by starting off with the Black Mountains. In these days of detailed road-books it would be a presumption to outline numerous routes of approach; but I may mention two routes from the English side to the Black Mountains district that each offer a splendid distant view of the countryside that awaits you. One proceeds from Worcester via Bromyard, Docklow (view), Leominster, Dilwyn, Willersley and Whitney to Hay; the other from Gloucester via Huntley, Mitcheldean, Ruardean (view, 13), Kerne Bridge, Whitchurch, Monmouth, Llantilio Crossenny and Abergavenny to Crickhowell.

KILPECK CHURCH

(Drawn by Roland W. Paul)

B

CHAPTER II

THE BLACK MOUNTAINS: GENERAL SURVEY, ETC.; THE FOUR RIDGES, AND THE VALLEYS OF THE RHIANGOLL, GRWYNE FAWR, GRWYNE FECHAN AND HONDDU

TRAVELLING from Malvern or Ledbury towards Hereford one descries on the western skyline a long, long ridge stretching indeterminately southwards but ending northwards in an escarpment so abrupt as to give the "edge" above it the appearance of a peak. The seeming peak is Hay Bluff, and the long hog's-back is the most easterly of the higher ridges of the Black Mountains: behind it hides the charming vale that shelters the roofless ruins of Llanthony Abbey. As one continues from Hereford up the mid Wye Valley towards Eardisley and Whitney, Clyro and Glasbury, other peaks and prominences come successively into view, till the nine-mile-long escarpment and the welter of tumbled foothills at its base stand wholly revealed. Good distant views of the outer eastern ridge are obtained from various other points of vantage —from the Gloucester-Ross route above Ross, for instance, or the high ground between Bromyard and Leominster, or Ruardean Hill in the Forest of Dean (13); even from certain heights on the Cotswold edge, such as Haresfield Beacon.

The Black Mountains of the Welsh-English Border[1] are a singularly unspoilt group of long and lofty ridges separated by valleys of diversified charm and descending steeply towards the Wye on the northern side, and on the southern less abruptly towards the Usk. In a looser sense the name will sometimes be extended to cover such supplemental eastern ridges and valleys as the Golden Valley, in which are situated two churches of unusual merit, those of Abbey Dore and Peterchurch (31, 32).

In this wider sense, then, the Black Mountains form a compact block, roughly rhomboidal or lozenge-shaped in plan,

[1] The term Black Mountain (singular) or the Welsh equivalent is given in maps to the group of peaks and moorlands between Carmarthen and the Towy: also, confusingly, to the ridge stretching from Hay Bluff.

10

15   THE "BRILLEY VIEW," THE NORTHERN EDGE OF THE BLACK MOUNTAINS ACROSS
THE WYE VALLEY

16 CWMYOY VILLAGE ABOVE THE HONDDU, ON THE SOUTHERN EDGE OF THE BLACK MOUNTAINS

with Talgarth, Crickhowell, Pontrilas (on the Hereford-Abergavenny road), and Bredwardine-on-Wye at the four corners. The escarpment facing the Wye runs from S.W. to N.E.: the ridges, seven in number, trend in a direction rather south of S.E. Anyone who first sees these grass-clad, heather-dappled heights abask in sunlight, or when fleecy clouds merely cast patches of shadow, may well be puzzled by the name—why *Black* Mountains? The answer is that from the Herefordshire side, except when the sun is pouring its rays on their nearer flank, they actually do look black, even under snow: the problem *solvitur aspiciendo*. In dull weather they stand out as a great dark-hued wedge against the grey of the sky (14); in all weathers, so soon as the sun is well past the meridian, the eastern ridge looms sombrely, passing from slate-blue monochrome to deeper hues as the daylight wanes, and, when there is a fine sunset, appearing theatrically silhouetted in inky tone against the western red. Perhaps it was the Saxons that first bestowed the name: it was almost always from this side that they saw these mountains: few of them ever crossed the Wye, and fewer still crossed it and returned.

Seen from the western side—from the long hill descending from Pen-y-genffordd, the road summit above Talgarth, to Tretower and Crickhowell, these mountains display typical moorland colouring, green of varied shades and russet brown diversified by dark patches of heather and blazing clumps of gorse. Yet one would most truly symbolize them by a deep, rich red. The whole mountain-block is composed of the Old Red Sandstone: all but one single peak-top that flaunts a white crest of limestone above Crickhowell and bears the appros priate name of Pen-cerrig-calch, "Chalkstones Head."

The four chief ridges and their valleys offer—to quote A. G. Bradley—"eighty square miles of complete, uncompromising solitude." Here the confirmed ridge-walker can indulge to the full his strange predilection: he can ridge-walk all day every day for a week and still find unfamiliar spurs to traverse. Here the solitary traveller may commune with God; or, if his will hath not so ambitious a working, he may take his ease and lie with Mother Earth. It is good, indeed, to loll awhile in a sheltered hollow on a couch of heath or bracken, drink in the moorland scents, and scan the distant view: from the various edges, when the skies are kind, you see displayed as on a magnified relief-map a great part of South Wales and most of Herefordshire. The Malverns and the Clee Hills beyond Ludlow close the eastern view: on the Welsh side the fantastic summits of the Brecon Beacons will arrest the gaze till it passes onward to dwell on the clear-cut angles of Carmarthen Van—one of Nature's more obvious contributions to Cubist art. The lower parts of the vales are easy of access; but if you prefer grappling with problems, if you are a porer over maps, an eager scanner of infrequent sign-posts, an adventurer on lanes that are always disappearing round corners—then the north side, the escarpment side, is the side for you; Hay, Clyro, Llowes, Glasbury, Three Cocks, Bronllys and Talgarth are your appropriate kicking-off places.

The minute topography of this northern side is unusually complicated and bewildering. The difficulties are largely due to the presence of a jumble of foothills and maze of little wooded valleys interposed between the escarpment proper and the south bank of the Wye. This welter of undulations and ravines, geologically the result of gradual erosion and detrition, forms a "dissected plateau" three to four miles wide; Talgarth, Three Cocks and Hay define its lower or northern edge, and it is crossed by a labyrinthine tangle of hard roads, green roads, cart tracks, lanes that are intermittently water-courses, field paths and shepherds' paths. But there are certain prominent landmarks by which you can generally steer or correct your aberrations. I shall not pretend that I know even half the practicable routes: after several years' acquaintance I am still in the learning stage. I can, however, provide a few "pointers" that may save others from needless waste of time and misdirection of energy; and to this task the ensuing pages shall be devoted.

The two highest summits, Waun Fach (2660 ft.) and Pen-y-gader Fawr (2624 ft.) lie remote on the *second* ridge, counting from the west. The most westerly, the Pen-allt-mawr ridge, overlooks the fine highway that runs down the beautiful Rhiangoll valley from Talgarth to Crickhowell. The next ridge is called by the map-makers the Pen-y-gader ridge. These two western ridges both start from the loftiest part of the escarpment, the plateau of Pen-y-Mallwyd, and enclose between them the loveliest and most sequestered of all the Black Mountains valleys, that of Grwyne Fechan. The eastern side of the Pen-y-gader ridge descends to the Grwyne Fawr valley.

On these western ridges you will see birds a-plenty—crows and jackdaws, peewits and pipits, and sometimes a hovering hawk or a raven, a pair of circling buzzards or a pack of grouse. Sheep and mountain ponies you will meet, but rarely a man, and then it will be a shepherd who begins greeting you in a high-pitched voice while still some distance away, a fashion perhaps derived unconsciously from ancestors who used this method of discerning friend from foe. There is in passing need for one warning; even those who are not new to mountains may be in danger from mist of the kind that materializes suddenly and will not lift. When caught by brooding mist, get down off the mountain at once; these ridges are not broad, and you can find the ridge-edge by continuously checking the direction of the wind, or win to safety by following running water—the merest trickle will do—downwards, an elementary fact which, to judge from occasional items in newspapers, is not consciously grasped by everyone whom one might expect to realize it. Finally, the best weather for distant views is showery weather with bright intervals.

A peculiarity of the Black Mountains is that from no road or valley on their immediate outskirts can you see their two highest summits, Waun Fach (2660 ft.) and Pen-y-gader Fawr (2624 ft.); they can be best approached from the road summit at Pen-y-genffordd (1066 ft.), three miles from Tal garth on the Crickhowell road, following a long ridge (Y Grib) to the undulating highest plateau.

Mynydd Troed, on the west side of Pen-y-genffordd, though under 2000 feet high, is a conspicuous landmark and offers extensive views. A lane starting from near the road-summit will bring you to a point whence you can see a track to the hill-crest gleaming red through bracken. From the top the western prospect centres on the Brecon Beacons but also includes, immediately below you, the gleaming level of Llangorse Lake; to north-west appears the sprawling bulk of the Eppynt hills, to northward the Radnorshire uplands with Radnor Forest in the background; best of all is the eastward view—the two western ridges of the Black Mountains, with Waun Fach and Pen-y-gader in lofty serenity, and the undulating outline of Y Grib descending from the escarpment to Castell-y-Dinas. If you concentrate your gaze on a point below Pen-y-gader you will remark a broad green track streaking the mountain side with a wavy diagonal: note it carefully, for it passes over the nearer (Penalltmawr) ridge by a deep notch, Bwlch Trumau, and is the short way to the Grwyne Fechan vale.

From Pen-y-Genffordd the highway goes on southward to Crickhowell. Few main roads offer such a continuous sequence of enchanting prospects. The temptation to speed offered by the excellent surface and the favourable gradient—downhill for five miles—should be nobly resisted. First, I would have you look out on the left, about a mile from the road-summit, for a lane descending to a sharp turn: you may know it by a straggly conifer at the far corner: this is the beginning of the short cut to the Grwyne Fechan vale. As you proceed, you will notice how the Penalltmawr ridge sends out a succession of rounded spurs on this side and how cultivation has mounted the intervening valleys. Watch presently for a thick wood dominated by three tall trees placed widely apart, one pair framing the distant Penalltmawr summit: this is perhaps the climax of the valley's beauty. On the left, Penalltmawr gives place to Pen-gloch-y-pibwr,[1] which rears a leonine crest high above Cwm-du, a village guarded by a fortress-like church tower. A *long* mile (see road-signs) brings you to Tretower, which justifies its name by showing you first a massive round tower, rising from the river bank below. This is an archæo-logical curiosity: a "juliet," built in King John's reign, inside and close up to one angle of a square Norman Keep, then already dilapidated as a result of Welsh energy. Tretower village lies amid clustering orchards, and beyond the village the road soon enters the Usk valley close to the beautiful Glan Usk park, and continues past the grounds of Gwernvale (p. 108) and along the foot of Pen-cerrig-calch into Crickhowell. A more adventurous route to this little town takes in also the Grwyne Fechan valley. The start is again made from Pen-y-genffordd, climbing at first steeply and then more easily to a notch in the ridge wall, Bwlch Trumau (2023 ft.) and follow-ing a long downward track to the Hermitage ridge, called after an appropriately named mansion near by. In its lower part the valley has fresh beauties in store. The great Pen-y-gader ridge throws out a succession of shapely spurs, showing clearly the terraced weathering at their summits, and often thickly wooded towards their bases: between them are dells or wider valleys showing an admixture of coppices and hedge-bordered fields. The road runs high up on the near side of the main valley, and a mile below Hermitage makes a long west-ward loop to cross a lateral valley, Cwm Banw. From the bridge at the head of the loop you look up the cwm to the leonine peak of Penalltmawr; beyond the bend you run along the flank of the limestone-crowned Pen-cerrig-calch, which is prolonged southwards by a spur ending in an extraordinary flat-topped eminence known as Table Mountain. On the latter is Crûg Hywel (from which Crickhowell is named), a

[1] "Peak of the piper's bell"; but what should a piper be doing with a *bell?*

17 THE HONDDU VALLEY NEAR CWMYOY, SOUTHERN EDGE OF
BLACK MOUNTAINS

18 A BRECONSHIRE FARM IN THE BLACK MOUNTAINS

19 LOOKING NORTHWARDS DOWN TOWARDS THE WYE VALLEY, FROM THE TRACK TO RHIW CWMSTABL
IN THE BLACK MOUNTAINS

prehistoric camp strengthened by ditch and masonry rampart; at its eastern foot lies Llanbedr, which our road presently approaches: hereabouts look left for a marvellous view presenting the Sugar Loaf as a perfect cone. The line of our road is continued by one running straight through to Crickhowell, fearfully steep towards the finish; but for scenery it is better to turn sharp left towards the church and, on reaching the latter, sharp right. Avoid two left turnings: the first is signposted "To Partrishow and Coalpit." Beyond the second you ascend a steep hill, from the top of which a wide prospect is enjoyed embracing the Vale of Usk and Crickhowell, with Mynydd Llangattock beyond them; to left, on this side of the vale, the Sugar-Loaf. Then follows a bracing descent to Crickhowell.

I have referred to the Grwyne Fach valley, though far less fully than its merits and my desire demand—because it has hitherto been unaccountably ignored—unsung by poets, unpainted by artists, unsnapped by Zeiss-Ikons, and dismissed in casual parentheses by otherwise admirable guide-books. This seems to me a strange lacuna. In my eyes this is the very phœnix and paragon of miniature valleys, a delightful epitome of the various perfections of moorland and upland dale and wooded gorge.

Turn we now to a sterner theme—the conquest of the escarpment. Between Hay Bluff on the east and Y Grib on the west, the escarpment is crossed by only three practicable ways: two of these meet at Capel-y-ffin in the Honddu valley, and are continued by the road to Llanthony; the third ascends the lofty Rhiw Cwmstabl[1] and descends the Grwyne Fawr gorge. There are several ways of approaching Rhiw Cwmstabl, all rather complicated; I shall describe that route which takes in the curious little church of Llanelieu (the ancient spelling was Llan Elyw and I fancy that this gives the proper pronunciation—Llan-elyoo). The most convenient starting-point is again Talgarth. Take the lane past the church; beyond the latter and a row of trim "villas" comes a fork, where you must descend to right, cross a bridge and mount again to meet an alternative route that starts on the west side of the "Tower" Hotel. The way presently passes the local Asylum (this should be on your *right*), then bears away to left. At the next road-fork follow the left arm. (The right arm leads past Sychnant farm

---

[1] *Cwmstabl* is simply "Constable" in Welsh dress: at least two of the de Bohuns, Earls of Hereford and Essex, held the office and title of Constable of England. Cf. "Lord Hereford's Knob."

to an unfenced track leading to the grassy avenue—see below —at the foot of Y Das.) Presently you pass through a gate and cross a stream, which keeps you company all the way to the church. To reach the latter you pass through a farmyard and mount a flight of steps. First you must ask for the key at the farmhouse: the door you tap is sheltered by a mediæval porch over which is inscribed a Vergilian tag—*Deus nobis haec otia fecit*. I have not discovered any clue to the farm's history, but Llanelieu Court, once a manor-house, was hereabouts. The church is a primitive-looking structure with a western bell-turret. The south doorway, framed in a timber porch, retains a mediæval door with original ironwork. The interior provides a surprise: a roughly fashioned rood-screen of timber bridged by a loft-floor, on which rests the back of the loft—a row of upright planks pierced with quatrefoil openings, possibly squints. Above comes the tie-beam of the roof, and above this again a tympanum crudely painted with a cross; the date is placed in the fourteenth century. On the reading-desk is a two hundred-year-old Book of Common Prayer in Welsh, rather dilapidated. Before you leave the churchyard, look towards the escarpment and you will see, rising in front of it as a sort of outer defence, a clear-cut massive spur shaped like a truncated pyramid. This is Y Das ("The Haycock"): note its position, since the track to Rhiw Cwmstabl starts over the *left* corner of it.

The next stage is tricky. Leave the farmyard by the rough road that passes the turret end of the church and continues with an ascent in the same direction. Arrived at more open and level ground continue forward towards Y Das, bearing left where the track forks, and ignoring cross-paths till you reach a regular cart track leading towards a farmhouse on right. Proceed in this direction a few paces, then make for a grassy avenue flanked by trees and bushes, which runs straight towards the nearer (eastern) base-angle of Y Das. At the farther end you espy the mountain track gleaming ruddily through bracken. Y Das can be reached directly from Pen-y-genffordd by the cart track skirting the base of Y Grib (see p. 13): it is rough and undulating, but *en route* offers delightful views of bracken-clad spurs of the escarpment, and of Y Das, cone-shaped from this angle.

Now comes a spell of strenuous climbing—a whole mile of roof-side gradients. (Here again the extra effort required for lugging a bicycle with you will be rewarded with compensating advantages later.) The track at first winds through high bracken, then mounts the flank of Y Das by steep pitches; higher up comes a series of zigzags. On the left is a deep gully, Cwm Cwmstabl, formed by a stream that has cut its way back into the escarpment. Its almost precipitous sides, scored and riven by countless storms, show bare red rock and patches of scree. This way of ascent gives you perhaps the most impressive "close-up" of the escarpment face, and when the zigzags begin you also get spacious prospects northwards over Radnorshire. As you approach the pass-summit (2267 ft.) the gradient eases, but the track grows rougher.

Arrived there, the traveller will need a short rest. The next step depends upon the object he has in view—whether it is the exploration of the escarpment or a ridge-walk or the descent of the Grwyne Fawr gorge. The actual highest point of the *edge*, Rhos Dirion (2338 ft.), is nearly a mile to left as you face south: the next pass, Rhiw Wen, is a mile beyond that, and on the farther side of it rises Lord Hereford's Knob. From Rhos Dirion the Fwddog ridge extends southwards between the Grwyne Fawr and Honddu valleys. Three-quarters of a mile due south of Rhiw Cwmstabl (for the edge makes a bend here) is Pen-y-manllwyn from which one may "ridge-walk" along Y Grib or along towards Pen-y-gader. If the objective is the Grwyne Fawr gorge, proceed steadily forward in the same general direction as previously. Indifferent walkers can be met by car at the reservoir.

Two miles of rough walking separates Rhiw Wen from the reservoir-head. For the first half-mile the track is merely a peaty path through a waste of bog, but later on the stream emerges, and to right front the turret-like summit of Pen-y-gader appears. At last the level expanse of the reservoir comes into sight ahead. In its deep hollow it seldom sparkles, and with its rim of confining concrete it is undisguisedly utilitarian. It is even well stocked with fish.

From the dam at the lake-foot a new road extends all the way down the valley: its surface is fair on the whole, though cyclists are troubled by the presence of loose grit. The valley quickly deepens into a miniature cañon, while the road descends more gradually, and is soon high above the stream. Apart from this, the first few miles lack thrills. A long descent ends in a bridge across the Grwyne; lower down, where the valley grows broader, there is an improvement: the Fwddog ridge, on your left, displays a series of shapely heights, and woods interspersed with pastures of flawless green ennoble the lower ground: there are signs of proprietorial care, this

C

being a portion of the far-flung Glan Usk estates. You flash through a tiny hamlet and plunge again into spreading woodlands, above and beyond which appears a moorland height shaped like a couchant lion. This is the famous Sugar-Loaf, seen from an unfamiliar angle.

If you wish to visit Partrishow Church, you must now prepare for the due performance of the preliminaries. You have first to seek the key at a certain farmhouse; then look out for a steep stony lane on right, which climbs up to a farmhouse. (The lane has a signpost at its entry, but is painted on one side only—the side looking *down* the valley.) At the farmhouse you will be agreeably and efficiently set on the right path to the church, a diminutive structure close at hand. The Puritan iconoclasts failed to find it—hardly a matter for surprise. It therefore retains undamaged a splendid rood-screen and loft of carved timber, dating from Henry VII's reign (29), and a rude font incised with the inscription "Menhir me fecit in tempore Genillin," the reference being to Genillin Foel, a prince of distant Powys in the eleventh century. The present building is mainly Tudor, but walled off at the west end is an anchorite's cell two hundred years older, which contains a stone altar marked with consecration crosses. Two similar altars remain on the west side of the screen. Some faint wall-paintings include a figure of Time complete with hour-glass and scythe. The name Partrishow—which sometimes appears in Italianate guise as Patricio—is said to be a corruption of Merthyr Isho (Isho's martyrdom) and to commemorate an unwholesome and officious hermit who rashly rebuked some lusty pagan prince.

The Grwyne Fawr gorge ends about three-quarters of a mile below the Partrishow turning. Here the stream is crossed by a bridge and then turns eastward to flow towards Llanbedr (see p. 15). After crossing the bridge you may either turn right for Fforest and the old Abergavenny-Crickhowell road or keep forward for the low pass to the Honddu valley and Pandy (see p. 24). The bridge is entitled Pont-yspig or Pont-y-escob: both mean Bishop's Bridge, the prelate referred to being Archbishop Baldwin, who made a preaching tour through Wales in 1188 in order to collect warriors for the Third Crusade. Giraldus Cambrensis—Gerald de Barri, the witty and versatile Archdeacon of Brecon, brilliant product of mixed Welsh and Norman parentage—accompanied Baldwin on this trip, which his famous *Itinerary* describes in detail.

We left the escarpment at the summit of Rhiw Cwmstabl.

20 LORD HEREFORD'S KNOB AND THE NORTHERN ESCARPMENT OF THE BLACK MOUNTAINS

21 LLANTHONY PRIORY IN THE HONDDU VALLEY OF THE BLACK MOUNTAINS

The next pass, Rhiw Wen (2032 ft.), crosses the escarpment one mile from its highest point (Rhos Dirion, p. 17), between the long N.E. slope of the latter (Rhiw-y-fan) and Lord Hereford's Knob (2263 ft.), which is rendered easy of recognition by the shape of its summit—a lofty round dome rising from a square plateau. It should be noted that the Knob—called in bastard Welsh Y Twmpa (the Tump)—does not terminate one of the great main ridges, but from it a triangle of high steep-sided moorland (see p. 20) projects southwards, separating the main Honddu valley, which lies on its east side, from the tributary dale known as Nant-y-bwch—a name equivalent in meaning to the Yorkshire *Buckden*. The ascent of Rhiw Wen itself is not very laborious, but the approach routes are complicated. The simplest way starts from Three Cocks. Turn up the lane beside the hotel, under the railway bridge, and at the first cross-lanes turn right so as to skirt Gwernyfed Park (notice fine vistas cut through fringing woods); keep forward to a junction with a road of better surface (this is the upper Hay-Talgarth road); turn along this to left, then shortly afterwards to right, along a road that runs quite straight towards a space between woods, skirting the park of Tregoyd, Lord Hereford's shooting-box. At the end of the straight piece bear right: the road now degenerates to a rough lane, knobbly and rutted, steep and serpentine, mounting between high banks. Presently the track becomes level and marshy, and you enter a straight piece between gates. Farther on avoid tracks to right and left but go forward through another gate, which admits to the open moor. Straight ahead you see, well marked on the escarpment face, a green road mounting diagonally as a shelf; this will take you to the pass-summit. Hence you can ascend Lord Hereford's Knob on left, a ten minutes' climb, or take a ridge-walk along the escarpment to right; or, if Llanthony is your objective, follow the track forward down the wild and lonely Nant-y-Bwch, until you join the main Hay-Llanthony track at Capel-y-ffin (see below). Once this dale had a fair sprinkling of inhabitants: it actually formed, with the adjacent moors, a little Lordship Marcher known as Glynbwch or Glanfach. The prominent peak seen far ahead on the Fwddog ridge is Chwarel-y-fan.

For the direct Hay-Llanthony route leave Hay by Forest Road (near the western end of the town), following it for two miles, until you reach a substantial farmhouse (New Forest Farm) opposite two contrasted trees, yew and haw-thorn. Some fifty yards onward a lane branches off to right this is the mountain road to Llanthony, and all you have to do is to keep to it, and look out for occasional cars. Hay Bluff soon comes into the near view, and away to right you see the long escarpment tapering away like a study in perspective; at this end of it Lord Hereford's Knob looms ever higher as you advance. Soon the road becomes a shelf, fairly level, running along the flank of Hay Bluff: it is no great matter to scramble up to the summit (2219 ft.), which offers spacious and diversified prospects on every side, and westward across the intervening ridges displays Pen-y-gader in the guise of a ruined tower. The shelf-road presently rounds an angle, and begins to mount towards the pass-summit, Bwlch-yr-Efengyl (1778 ft.), which lies at the head of the deep cwm of the Digedi brook. (The lane up along the latter from Llanigon near Hay peters out beyond the Pennant farmhouse.) The name Bwlch-yr-Efengyl (Gospel Pass) perhaps indicates that periodically religious gatherings were convened here by the Llanthony monks. But how draughty!

Beyond the bwlch the track descends, with undulations, along the flank of the triangular moor mentioned above. On the left is a wild cwm from the recesses of which the infant Honddu trickles down to become the stream of an ever-deepening valley; on the farther side of the latter rises the long ridge running south from Hay Bluff—the Black Mountain, specially so termed by the map-makers. The unfenced part of the road ends at an awkwardly-placed gate. From this point the lane narrows and is bordered by high hedges—surface indifferent, here and there definitely bad—till at Capel-y-ffin it is joined by the track from Rhiw Wen.

A little way up the latter stands the "monastery" built by "Father Ignatius," an eccentric character—who was ordained as an Anglican clergyman and soon acquired some social notoriety by his handsomely striking person, forcible and fluent oratory and extreme High-Churchism. Funds supplied largely by women of means enabled him—the Reverend Lester Lyne (as he was till he assumed his self-bestowed paternal title) to establish in this remote but beautiful spot an Anglican bisexual coenobitic community; this he had the effrontery to name Llanthony Abbey: the genuine Llanthony *Priory* is four miles down the vale.

The little hamlet of Capel-y-ffin (Boundary Chapel—there actually is a tiny chapel-of-ease here (41): the boundary is that between Brecon and Monmouthshire) lies about two and a half miles below the bwlch and three and a half miles above

Llanthony; but from this point there is an excellent road to the very end of the vale. This lower and broader part is distinguished by the title of Vale of Ewyas, a name derived from the important Marcher Lordship held in Norman times by the powerful de Lacy family, one of whom founded the priory in Henry I's reign. The road runs high above the stream: the great ridge above its farther bank is in view all the way; pastures, woods and scattered farmsteads fill the foreground. The Fwddog ridge, on right, is hidden by steep foothills, but comes into sight where the valley curves again lower down. You cross the Honddu a little short of the priory, the actual approach to which is a short steep lane on left. Looking hence down the vale one cannot but admire the rich variety of scenery (21); though the brothers Wade expatiate on its "bleakness" and "sombreness."[1]

From the head of the approach you cross a yard, bounded on right by a little Norman church, and after passing through a gate walk across a lawn to the grass-floored nave of the priory church: the north arcade is the best-preserved part of the building. On the left are portions of the two west towers (22): the southern of the pair, together with the adjacent prior's lodging, has been repaired and extended to serve as an inn. To east of the nave two sides of the central tower still stand, and fragments of the choir; of the transepts the southern is the best preserved; a pair of lancets remain in its south wall, and the east wall is pierced by an arch that led into a chapel. To south of this transept is the chapter house, now used as a garage. The building is assigned to the period of transition from Norman to Early English; it is not the original church but dates from a rebuilding begun towards the end of the twelfth century. The monks (Augustinian Canons) who were planted here sighed for more civilized surroundings from the very beginning, and the sigh was later intensified to a despairing cry: what with mountains, storms, wolves and wild Welsh neighbours, they regarded Llanthony as a premature Purgatory. In Stephen's reign the bulk of them migrated to a new priory established for them at Gloucester, the scanty remains of which now stand forlorn amid railway sidings.

At the inn among the ruins—the Llanthony Abbey Hotel —you can obtain comfortable and moderate-priced accommodation: good country fare, good fires (they are seldom not needed), good beer and cider and strong waters, soporific

[1] In the *Little Guide for Monmouthshire*.

beds; some day there will be bathrooms. The view of the eastern ridge, as seen through the nave arcade, is pleasantly unusual. Mountain paths lead over Rhiw Arw, a peak of that ridge, to Longtown and the Monnow valley, to Oldcastle and, by a "shelf" path along the farther side of Hatteral Hill, to Pandy. (Hatteral Hill is the south-eastern portion of the ridge.) By ascending the deep ravine conspicuous on the western side of the valley you reach the twin rounded heights of Bal Mawr and Bal Bach and may look across the Grwyne Fawr to Pen-y-gader.

In a wood on the hillside above the priory stands—or was standing till recently—a ruined barn, sole remnant of a mansion begun but never completed by the eccentric man of letters, Walter Savage Landor, whose brief connection with the Vale of Ewyas was a tragic-comic interlude in its history. In 1809 Landor, who had inherited considerable properties in the Midlands (he did not, however, belong to the then exclusive "landowning" class), sold these in order to purchase the Llanthony estate. His mind was filled with grandiose schemes for turning it into a sort of feudal domain, schemes foredoomed to failure not only through rustic conservatism but by his own cantankerous disposition, blind arrogance and lack of business capacity. For the rôle of county magnate, which he now essayed to play, he was quite unfitted, whether by breeding, tastes or character. County people and Church dignitaries alike cold-shouldered him: he showed *trop de zèle*. Local authorities would not dance to his piping. The tenant-farmers and peasantry of the estate refused to comport themselves as his villeins and serfs: hence his vilification of the Welsh. Finally, serious financial difficulties compelled him to relinquish control of the property to trustees; and in 1814 he relieved Llanthony of his ridiculous though disturbing presence—not, unfortunately, before much damage had been done to the abbey ruins by his tinkering.

Below Llanthony the scenery of the Honddu valley loses much of its wildness, but derives grace from cultivation and planned effects, among which are broad bands of woodland striping hill-sides from crest to foot. In three miles or so look up across the valley for the first sight of Cwmyoy church tower. Hatteral Hill separates at its extremity into two massive spurs with a hollow between them: the hollow is Cwm Yoy, but Cwmyoy village is perched high up on the end of the nearer spur—very precariously, since it just

22 THE RUINS OF THE TRANSITIONAL FABRIC OF LLANTHONY PRIORY CHURCH, DESERTED IN THE THIRTEENTH CENTURY

23 THE FIRST FURROW: PLOUGHING NEAR PANDY, LOOKING TO
HATTERAL HILL IN THE BLACK MOUNTAINS

24 VIEW IN THE GRWYNE FECHAN VALLEY OF THE BLACK
MOUNTAINS, LOOKING TO THE PENALLTMAWR RIDGE

escaped being swept away by a landslip of which the deep notch just above it is a reminder.

Beyond the Queen's Head Inn watch for a lane going off to right: this is the short cut to the Grwyne valleys, big and little, to Partrishow, and to Llanbedr and Crickhowell (see p. 15). At last you pass under a railway bridge and approach a little village with a long name—Llanvihangel Crucorney. Motorists and cyclists returning towards Hay have a choice of routes: they may turn left just beyond the railway and proceed up the Monnow valley by way of Longtown and Craswall— but the descent to the Wye valley is steep, stony and mult-angular (see p. 34)—or join the Abergavenny-Hereford road at the village and make for the Golden Valley via Pandy and Pontrilas.

THE CHAINED CARP, PETERCHURCH CHURCH
(Drawn by H. T. Timmins).

CHAPTER III

THE BLACK MOUNTAINS (EASTERN POR-TION): VALLEYS OF THE DORE ("GOLDEN" VALLEY), MONNOW AND ESCLEY

PANDY and Pontrilas, mentioned in the final paragraphs of the previous chapter, are strategic points of importance to the conscientious topographer: both are meeting-places of several roads, and both have stations on the branch-line linking Hereford with Abergavenny. Neither is more than a mere hamlet. Llanvihangel Court, near Pandy, a large Tudor mansion of stone, presents a handsome gabled front to passers-by: the back of the building, still more attractive, and an avenue of firs in the grounds are seen by the favoured few. The Skyrrid Inn, farther south, genuinely retains the interior arrangement of pre-railway days. Some striking views of Skyrrid Fawr are obtainable hereabouts.

The main road from Pandy to Pontrilas is comparatively dull, though its excellent surface invites to speed: the funny little church between road and river towards the end of this stage is that of Llangua, where there was once an alien priory. For a less direct route that includes two buildings of unusual interest, follow the Longtown road either from Pandy or (see p. 23) from Llanvihangel Crucorney as far as cross-roads half a mile from the former, and there turn right as if for Walterstone. You can cross the Monnow immediately above its junction with the Honddu; on the farther bank of the former stands the Tudor farmhouse of Allt-yr-ynys, which was the original cradle of a family that for four hundred years has been prominent in the public life of England—the Sitsyllts or Cecils, the latter being the Welsh name in English dress. The first of the family to attain high distinction was Robert Cecil, Lord Burleigh: the great Queen who found in him her most trusted and able counsellor belonged, like him, to a stock that originated in petty Welsh squires.

Having pored upon the brook that babbles by, now mount the hill that passes immediately behind Allt-yr-ynys. The road rises steadily to Walterstone Common, passing a well-marked

camp formed by a triple ring of earthworks; then undulates
gently till a steeper dip and ascent herald the approach to
Rowlstone Church. This building, easily identified by its
pyramid-capped west tower, is mainly of Norman date (1130).
The south doorway and the chancel arch are worth close examination. The former has a carved tympanum representing
Christ in Majesty seated and wearing distinctly Oriental garb,
with two angels on either side flying *downward* to fulfil His
bequests. Each angel grasps with both hands a *vesica* or oval
frame surrounding the central figure. The handle of the door
below is ornamented with a pair of twined serpents whose
heads are separated by the knop—a pretty piece of workman-
ship. Adjacent to the capitals of the chancel-arch responds
are panels each carved
with two figures, one
an angel, the other pro-
bably St. Peter; on the
south panel the figures
are shown heads down-
wards, as drawn (p. 27).
The imposts are pro-
longed to meet the
outer walls and are
carved with foliage and
figures of birds, prob-
ably cocks. From the
north and south chan-

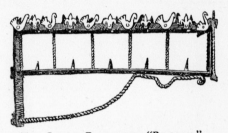

THE CANDLE BRACKET OR "PRICHET,"
ROWLSTONE CHURCH

(Drawn by H. T. Timmins)

cel walls extend curious brackets of wrought iron. Each
is formed by two horizontal bars separated by twisted
uprights dividing it into five open panels; in each panel
a short upright spike projects from the lower bar and
there is a ring opposite it on the upper bar; the spikes
were intended for candles, the rings to hold them in place.
The upper bars are ornamented with *fleurs-de-lis* and birds,
cocks on the north side, swans on the south, cut out of metal
plates. The cocks here and on the imposts symbolize the
patron saint of the church, St. Peter. These candle brackets—
long supposed to be "riddel" or curtain brackets—are unique
in this country.

From Rowlstone a pleasant descent brings the traveller into
the main Hereford road at Pontrilas: to reach the Golden
Valley he must take the next turning left, for Ewyas Harold
(below). The Ewyas district, which after the Norman Conquest
was a Lordship Marcher embracing the eastern half of the

D

Black Mountains (using that term in the wider sense), had enjoyed unusual privileges from the time of the later Saxon kings. The neighbouring district of Archenfield, which was bounded by the Wye, the Monnow and the Worm Brook, was similarly populated and enjoyed similar privileges, guaranteed in this case by a still extant ordinance of Athelstan's reign. As a Lordship Marcher, Ewyas, with its castles of Ewyas Harold and Ewyas Lacy (Longtown), was held for many generations by the de Lacys, then passed with the ultimate de Lacy heiress to the Genvilles, and finally through another marriage was added with Ludlow to the domains of the all-absorbing Mortimers.

Lovers of scenery are advised to travel up rather than down the Golden Valley on a first trip. Ewyas Harold, the first village reached from Pontrilas, though hardly attractive, is of some historical importance as containing the site of a "castle" erected by one of Edward the Confessor's Norman protegés. This was "rebuilt" by William FitzOsborn, whom the Conqueror made Earl of Hereford; it was held under him by Alured of Marlborough. The castle was merely a motte-and-bailey defended by moats and timber stockades, with garrison quarters of timber: the earthworks still remain just beyond the north side of the village, close to the road leading via Dulas to Longtown. (Dulas, by the way, has a church noted for its store of Jacobean carved woodwork.)

The road to Abbey Dore starts by mounting a hill, and going in this direction you reach the church of Abbey Dore before the village; a good thing, since the latter is ramshackle and unsightly. By contrast, the interior of Abbey Dore Church is a feast of beauty: the huddled, rather lop-sided appearance of the exterior is due to the destruction of the nave and the location of the tower between the south transept and chancel aisle. Perhaps the best external feature is the south façade of the transept.

The church is that of a Cistercian monastery founded in the middle of the twelfth century by Robert of Ewyas, a great-grandnephew of Edward the Confessor. The present remains—transepts, each with an eastern chapel, chancel and ambulatory (or continuous chancel aisle)—date from an early rebuilding carried out between 1180 and 1210. Funds for this laudable purpose were easily raised by the abbot of that period—one Adam, some startling instances of whose roguery —and of his monks' gluttony and wine-bibbing—are attested by the good Catholic priest Giraldus Cambrensis, whose

25   THE WEST SIDE OF STOCKLEY HILL: THE GOLDEN VALLEY AND THE BLACK MOUNTAINS
WITH PETERCHURCH SPIRE

26 PETERCHURCH AND THE GOLDEN VALLEY

strictures are supported by the authority of the grave and judicious Walter Map.

When at last a monarch of Welsh descent restored to secular uses the accumulations of centuries of fraud, this Abbey of Dore with its endowments was bestowed upon one of the "esquires of the King's body," John Scudamore, member of an old Marcher family descended from a de Lacy heiress. During the next hundred years the nave and choir, and most of the monastic buildings were demolished—the stumps of the piers of the nave arcades remain, together with one arch—but in 1633 another John Scudamore, afterwards first Viscount Scudamore, a man who did valuable service in improving the strain of Herefordshire orchards and the breed of Herefordshire cattle, handed over the remaining portions of the structure to serve as a parish church, at the same time reroofing it, adding the tower, and providing fittings and furniture of richly carved woodwork.

CARVING ON A CHANCEL-ARCH CAPITAL, ROWLSTONE
(Drawn by H. T. Timmins)

Abbey Dore Church is a notable example of the pure Early English style in its richer form: the three presbytery arcades (for there is a transverse arcade at the east end) and the tall lancet windows of the clerestory above, the lofty arches of the crossing between the transepts, and the enriched arches leading from the latter into the ambulatory, all evoke the admiration of enthusiasts. The ambulatory (31) is divided into bays, of which there is on the east side a double range divided by piers, making sixteen in all: each is covered by a ribbed vault, and the exterior walls are pierced by lancets in every bay. The piers of the ambulatory are formed each of eight clustered shafts, whose varied capitals are among the finest examples of "stiff-stalked" foliage known.

The timber roofs are attributed to John Abel, the "King's Carpenter," who designed the half-timbered market halls of Leominster and Ledbury and the "Old House" at Hereford. The finely-carved woodwork fittings include an elaborate (perhaps rather vulgar?) chancel-screen (30), a restrained but effective west gallery, Laudian altar-rails, handsome pews and desks, and some panelling on the presbytery walls (west bays). The painted glass of the presbytery eastern lancets dates from the seventeenth century, but its colour-tones are of striking beauty: there are fragments of earlier glass in the south transept chapel.

The next point of interest as you ascend the vale is the little parish church of St. Faith, Bacton, to reach which you take a left turn off the main road. Entering by the south porch you see on the opposite wall an elaborate Tudor monument showing Queen Elizabeth in stiff raiment and starchy ruff, wearing her regalia and looking rather grumpy; and kneeling at her feet, humble and demure, her faithful maid-of-honour, Blanche Parry, a relative of the Vaughans of Bredwardine and Tretower. The figures are in high relief, and in an elaborate inscription Blanche is made to testify that in spite of manifold temptations offered by naughty courtiers she lived and died a maiden in the service of a maiden Queen. On the same wall, in a glazed frame, is an altar frontal embroidered with a botanical and zoological miscellany by the spinsterish Blanche. From Bacton steep devious lanes meandering towards the Escley valley lead to the wood-embowered little church of St. Margaret, which contains a richly carved Perpendicular screen and panelled rood-loft of much distinction.

Beyond the Bacton turn you join a superior road coming in from Hereford: the wooded slope seen on the skyline to right shelters Monnington Court, close to which is an oval motte, probably the site of a vanished mansion of the Scudamores—though some identify this with Chapel Farm close by. It is important to notice that it was here, at *this* Monnington Court—*not* at Monnington-on-Wye—that (if the tradition is credible) Owen Glyndwr remained in safe obscurity during his uneventful closing years. The error of locating his place of refuge at Monnington-on-Wye has been repeated by one writer after another; some of them have actually identified his tomb in Monnington-on-Wye churchyard. Even the veteran A. G. Bradley, paragon and exemplar of chroniclers of the March, falls into this trap. An excusable lapse, for this Monnington—Monnington Straddel—is remote and little known; yet the Monnington manor held by the Scudamore who married Glyndwr's daughter Alice was Monnington Straddel: the Wye-side Monnington was at the time in question (1415–17) a manor of the Audleys and lay in a district then already Anglicized and strongly anti-Glyndwr.

Straddel, the Norman name for the Golden Valley, is a corruption of Welsh *ystrad*, which can mean *strath* as well as *street*, though the latter meaning is not inappropriate here, since the Roman road from Abergavenny to Kenchester crossed the valley near Abbey Dore. What, then, is the origin of the title "Golden Valley"? The pedagogic explanation is that the Normans confused the Welsh *dwr* (water) with the French *d'or*: this perhaps accounts for Abbey Dore, but the original form of Dorstone (at the head of the vale) was *Torchestone*. "Golden Valley" perhaps dates from the not remote era of similar christenings, of "Fairy Glens," "Pixies' Pools" and the like: there are two "Golden Valleys" in Gloucestershire, one of which was so entitled—quite inappropriately—by Queen Victoria.

Leaving now these tremendous trifles, we continue up the valley, which often *is* golden with the honey-sweet efflorescence of gorse and broom, or the ripening cheeks of russet apples, and the tawny sheen of cornfields, till presently a byway on left drops down to two little villages, Vowchurch and Turnastone, separated only by the stream and the railroad. The churches of these two villages are small, and each has a western bell-turret, that of Vowchurch being of timber framing and white plaster, with a high pyramidal cap (34), that of Turnastone squat and weather-boarded. The Vowchurch edifice has a remarkable assortment of carved timber-work of the Stuart period, screen, chairs, altar-rails, choir benches, and a beechen chalice, and an amazingly elaborate queen-post roof mainly of the same date (two bays are three centuries older), supported by massive posts set against the walls. At one side of the churchyard is a timber-framed Tudor house, the Old Vicarage (35), now divided into tenements. Thomas ap Harry (d. 1522), commemorated in the neighbouring Turnastone Church by a white marble slab with incised figures, was related to Blanche Parry of Bacton. The Carolean pulpit in Turnastone Church shows grace and restraint. When I visited Vowchurch my examination of the woodwork was curtailed by the sudden intrusion of a flock of little boys and girls, all chattering like starlings, who came to see what I was up to. These children differed from the usual throngs that gather round the student of rural churches in that they were all dripping wet and clad in bathing dresses, decent of cut but dazzling of hue.

But I must hurry you along to Peterchurch, which offers more dignified attractions. While still quite distant you descry a "Heaven-ypointed finger," the slender Decorated spire of St. Peter's Church (25, 26). When you reach the building you find that it has an apsidal east end, but this and the Norman south doorway with its original door hardly prepare you for the remarkable interior (32). This is of little-altered Norman work and is divided into four compartments—nave, choir, presbytery and apsidal sanctuary—by plain round arches resting on imposts; several deeply-splayed Norman lights remain, including the three original windows of the apse. The Norman font is of unusual pattern—a heavy cup-shaped bowl on a base of almost equal diameter, the junction of the parts being defined by a thick cable ornament. On the south wall is an antiquarian puzzle: a plaster panel showing in relief the crudely-coloured figure of a large carp wearing a golden chain (p, 23). This is the modern replica of a cast known to have been here since before 1700. The most determined symbolist can hardly find a mystic significance in this strange anomaly. Is it, perhaps, a figure dedicated in gratitude after the ancient Greek fashion by some pious angler?

A cross road at the south end of Peterchurch village leads towards the Escley valley via Urishay Castle and in the other direction to Wellbrook Manor and Stockley Hill (see p. 35). Urishay Castle is now represented by a farmhouse, but close by is a motte-and-bailey: on the motte stand remnants of a Jacobean mansion; within the bailey is the chapel, now renovated, of an earlier moated dwelling. Dorstone is a large, cheerful and prosperous-looking village. The wholly rebuilt church retains, among the relics of its predecessor, a thirteenth-century "coffin-chalice" (chalice of pewter buried with a priest) and a window-sill carved with an inscription recording the endowment of a chantry in 1256 by one John Brito. A conspicuous landmark on the ridge above Dorstone is a notable cromlech known as Arthur's Stone, the remnant of a long barrow, to-day rather blatantly railinged and noticeboarded. For the easier road to Hay from Dorstone bear right at the fork beyond the village. Notice presently Bach, an eighteenth-century farmhouse with buildings on each side of the road. Approaching Hay you have on right the demesne of The Moor, a modern mansion; on left, high in the woods, the prehistoric Mouse Castle (see p. 31).

The Golden Valley is the easternmost of the outer Black Mountains valleys: it has been here given precedence over the other two, the Escley and Upper Monnow valleys, because it contains so many definite points of interest. Of the three

27 LONGTOWN CASTLE ON ITS MOTTE, BY THE OLCHON BROOK,
BLACK MOUNTAINS

28 GRANGE FARM, ABBEY DORE, IN THE GOLDEN VALLEY

29   THE XV CENTURY: THE ROOD LOFT, PARTRISHOW

30   THE XVII CENTURY: JOHN ABEL'S SCREEN, ABBEY DORE

CONTRASTS IN SCREEN DESIGN

eastern valleys and their bounding ridges it may be said generally that they lack the grand proportions, vast solitudes and scarce-tamed wildness of their western neighbours. But they are well-timbered and diligently cultivated, a fair amount of fruit being grown; and since their fertility and the soft charm of their scenery recommended them to the taste both of the Normans and of the Tudor-period *nouveaux riches*, they abound in Norman mottes, castle ruins and churches, and Tudor mansions and cottages. In this respect the Golden Valley takes precedence over the others.

Yet the touch of wildness is not wholly wanting: the long ridge stretching from Hay Bluff to Hatteral Hill is ever in the background, filling the western sky; closely imminent, indeed, as you travel the road between Longtown and Hay. Moreover, from just south of Hay Bluff this "Black Mountain" ridge throws out a long narrow spur towards Longtown, known as Black Hill and, farther south, Crib-y-Garth. Ridge and spur, and the deep Olchon valley they enclose, belong essentially to the moorland. The more easterly ridges are for the most part cultivated or wooded to their summits, and seldom overtop the 1000-foot mark, except at their northern ends, where Cefn Hill (1593 ft.) terminates the ridge between the Monnow and Escley valleys, and Vagar Hill between the Escley and the Golden Valleys: the outer rampart that guards the latter on the east and drops down abruptly to the Wye ends north-wards in Merbach Hill (1045 ft.).

The Escley and upper Monnow valleys can be conveniently explored on a single circular trip from the Hay district. The use of *small* cars is feasible, but portions of the roads on the Hay side are awkward and very rough: the tramp-cum-cycle method is more satisfactory. To get the best effects follow the Escley for the outward journey. Leave Hay, then, by the Bredwardine and Hereford road; avoid the Cusop turning but take the next lane going to right. You soon pass near a large farm significantly named Llidiart-y-Waun (Moor Gate), and the lane grows fairly steep. The wood on the hilltop to left conceals Mouse Castle, a small but finely-situated prehistoric earthwork. When the lane forks, resist the temptation to take the left-hand easier way, and keep straight ahead. The track soon zigzags over the flank of Cusop Hill, but later the gradient eases and you grow conscious of cool moorland airs; signs of civilization become more scanty as you round the hollow whence springs the infant Dore. A mile beyond a onely farm you reach the road summit (1400 ft.) and then enjoy—if you are cycling—a fairly level run along a peaty track barely sheltered by stunted trees; or you may halt and look over the shoulder of Cefn Hill to Hay Bluff, clear-cut and looking monstrous high from this angle; in the deep intervening hollow you catch a reddish gleam that is the Craswall-Hay road. Beyond Ty-uchaf (Upper House) the descent begins, rough and steep at first, but pleasanter after you pass the next house, Llan Rosser, where you hear the prattling of the Escley brook on your left.

At Michaelchurch Escley a cross-lane leads left to a bridge and the inn, right to Michaelchurch Court, Elizabethan with gables half-timbered in various patterns. Here the main road improves: soon you pass the church, which like most churches of this district rewards the conscientious sightseer with a surprise: the nave north wall displays a fifteenth-century wall-painting in crude colours—a large figure of Christ surrounded by a medley of craftsmen's tools and domestic implements among which a gridiron and a frying pan are discernible, thus recalling the Cornish "Christ of the Trades" paintings.

As you travel onward look across to right for the continuation of Black Mountain—Rhiw Arw and Hatteral Hill. At the foot of a long descent you cross the Monnow just above its junction with the Escley. A little farther, and you meet the Craswall road at a sharp angle close to the principal inn of Longtown: the single road proceeding hence southwards joins the Hereford-Abergavenny road at Pandy. Once when I was enjoying a late tea at this inn a friendly farmer who had dropped in for a preliminary pint discoursed to me eloquently of fruit-trees, of precautions against insect-pests, of plaguy storms, of markets, of ignorant Whitehall folk who couldn't tell a Golden Russet from a Quarenden, blast their alliterative eyes! For you must know that hereabouts, just as all round Evesham and Pershore, in pubs and places where men do congregate the talk is all of fruit and orchards—highly technical talk, hardly understanded of the layman. This farmer was an Englishman of Herefordshire; his name, the familiar Welsh patronymic that I bear. Trace back his ancestry and you might come to that Ewyas stock of which I wrote just now.

A big vivacious fellow I met here on another occasion assured me that years ago a vicar of Longtown periodically used to empty all the local chapels by the sheer force of his oratory, which would attract not only his own flock but everybody in his own and neighbouring parishes. Strange as it may seem, this heterogeneous multitude used to hasten to

31   THE RETROCHOIR, ABBEY DORE
CHURCH

32   THE NORMAN INTERIOR OF PETERCHURCH
IN THE GOLDEN VALLEY

CONTRASTS IN DESIGN: EARLY GOTHIC AND ROMANESQUE

c

33   THE WOODED OUTER EDGE OF THE GOLDEN VALLEY AT STOCKLEY HILL

church every Low Sunday in order to hear him preach a long, long sermon. Not an ordinary kind of sermon. It took the form of a general critical survey of the morals, manners, appearance, personal adornment, and habits (too social or anti-social) of his parishioners, male and female, recently deceased or alive and kicking. The defunct he mentioned by name, the living by implication, subtle but perspicuous.

Before starting on the return route any keen antiquarian should stroll down the Pandy road to a bridge (Pont Hendre) over the Olchon, just beyond which, on the right, is a prominent motte-and-bailey—probably the original "castle" of Ewyas Lacy erected by Roger de Lacy, to whom the Conqueror gave leave to constitute this district a Marcher Lordship. In the opposite direction, the road to Craswall begins with a long stiff climb up the single street of the strung-out village of Longtown—an appropriate name. (Ribbon development is no new thing.) At the top of the village comes a surprise: on the left of the road a massive round tower and pieces of curtain wall, the longest of them pierced with a gateway arch, crown a steep-sided motte (27) and on the opposite side is a tangle of earthworks partly covering the site of the original bailey. These are relics of a Norman castle built towards the end of the twelfth century to supersede the older motte near Pont Hendre. Beyond the castle comes the long undulating ascent of the Monnow valley to Craswall, five miles away. On this stretch of road you have the steep-sided spur of Crib-y-Garth looming ever higher above you. A lane turning steeply to left soon after you leave Longtown leads to the lonely, primitive little church of Llanveynoe, and is continued as a rough track along Crib-y-Garth; another track leads from the church into the wild Olchon valley and may be followed by the "stout pedestrian" up that valley and over the flank of Hay Bluff to the New Forest Farm track (p. 19).

After the main road has passed two or three groups of houses that are parts of Craswall—there is no actual village—it reaches a corner which luckily has a large A.A. signpost pointing the way to Hay: you turn sharp to right past the Bull's Head Inn and at once cross the infant Monnow. There is a lane going off to left from the signpost: it looks as though it might take you to the foot of Hay Bluff. And indeed it *will* lead you, in intense discomfort, to Coed Major farm, some mile away from its eastern foot; but if after that you are able to find your way through a tangle of tracks, hillsides, gullies and thickets to Hay, you will reach your destination a thinner and infinitely thirstier man.

Even the good road that takes you on from the Bull's Head, though unmistakable, is far from easy going. It makes a long loop, then ascends steadily to a farmstead, beyond which it is gated and grass-grown; then comes a run over open moor from which Hay Bluff is seen to full advantage. Before the road-summit (1450 ft.) is reached, a pathway on right may (with difficulty) be found leading to Craswall Priory, but the ruins, scanty and neglected, are of interest only to antiquarians.

The descent from the road-summit is of a kind to demand all your attention if you are cycling or driving a car. Parts of the route are fairly steep and there are several sudden dips and awkward turns, including one true hairpin bend. You run along the edge of the thickly wooded Dulas glen, which later becomes the Cusop dingle: the scenery is attractive, but to study it satisfactorily one must walk. At New Forest Farm (p. 19) the gradient eases, and during the final drop to Hay you may enjoy the wide prospect across the Wye valley to the Radnorshire uplands.

THE VOLCA CHAMBER, KINGSLAND CHURCH
(Drawn by H. T. Timmins)

34 VOWCHURCH CHURCH REFLECTED IN THE RIVER DORE,
GOLDEN VALLEY

35 THE OLD VICARAGE AT VOWCHURCH, IN THE GOLDEN
VALLEY, NOW COTTAGES

36 AN EVENING VIEW ACROSS HEREFORDSHIRE, LOOKING TO WORMSLEY HILL
WITH THE PYON HILLS TO LEFT

CHAPTER IV

THE MID WYE AND MONNOW VALLEYS,
INCLUDING HAY, BREDWARDINE,
MADLEY, KILPECK, AND THE CASTLES
OF THE TRILATERAL

THIS chapter will be chiefly occupied with the country surrounding the northern and eastern outskirts of the Black
Mountains; more especially, with places of special interest or
beauty lying on or between the two main roads from Hereford
to Glasbury. The "castles of the Trilateral" were Grosmont
and Skenfrith, both in the Monnow valley, and White Castle,
nearer Abergavenny. This *triangle* of fortresses was of particular importance in the scheme of Border defence against Welsh
attacks, and as few of the Lords Marchers could be com-
pletely trusted, was after Henry III's reign retained for the
royal Duchy of Lancaster. As a measure of safety the first
Yorkist King, Edward IV, rendered all three castles unten-
able. The Herefordshire "black-and-white" villages lie mostly
north of the *northern* Hereford-Hay route, and will be the
subject of a later chapter.

Excellent comprehensive views of the Herefordshire lowland may be obtained from the eastern slopes of roads linking
the Golden Valley with the Wye Valley. Of these, the byways
from Abbey Dore to Thruxton and from Bacton to Kingstone
cross the pleasant Grey Valley; the route (part of B4348) from
Vowchurch turning to Kingstone passes near Monnington
Straddel (p. 28) and offers a splendid retrospective view of the
Black Mountains. The remaining pair, Stockley Hill (see p. 30)
and the Dorstone-Bredwardine lane, call for fuller description. Stockley Hill is a short-cut from Peterchurch to the Wye
Valley. Soon after leaving Peterchurch it passes Wellbrook
Manor, which retains a chimney stack and some interior work
of the fourteenth century. The view from the top of Stockley
Hill (33, 37, 25) is said to "embrace parts of six counties," but
this stupid formula does not express its real value, which lies
rather in its quality; on the farther side the lane descends
between high banks topped by hedges wherein dog-roses and

honeysuckle run riot, and draped in a careless profusion of humbler wild flowers. Framed within this tangled broidery gleams the rich Herefordshire champaign, diversified at well-spaced intervals with those graceful isolated hills (36), mantled in woods from base to summit, that are characteristic of these Border lowlands all the way from Bishop's Castle in Salop to Caerwent near Severn Sea. The lane that takes one from Dorstone to near Bredwardine over the southern prolongation of Merbach Hill is steeper and stonier, but displays an equally varied distant prospect and, close by, reveals noble trees in Moccas deer-park. At the summit it passes the approach to Arthur's Stone.

On nearing the foot of Stockley Hill it is best to bear left and join the Hereford-Hay road at Tyberton. Here is a Renaissance church of red brick; handsome conifers fringing the churchyard form a background for a fourteenth-century cross with carved panelled head. There is a similar cross at Madley, some three miles towards Hereford. Madley Church is one of the most remarkable of the whole Border. The north porch is a relic *in situ* of a Norman cruciform church of which it was the north transept, and which was replaced piecemeal by a much larger Early English structure. The chancel of the latter made way in turn for the present Decorated apsidal chancel (notice the ball-flower) and the vaulted crypt below it; last of all, about 1330, the south (Chilston) Chapel was added. The embellishments of the interior include Decorated triple sedilia, chancel-stalls with carved misericords, a Jacobean pulpit and, at the east end of the north aisle, a beautiful panelled box-pew. The Garnons and Willison monuments, the latter of which is "signed" by its maker John Gildo, merit careful inspection; but the rarest treasure of the church is the early fourteenth-century painted glass in the windows of the apse; particularly, in the east window, three panels of a Jesse window, and in the tracery quatrefoils, shields with the arms of Bohun and Warenne.

In the other direction from Tyberton, towards Hay, the road soon approaches Moccas deer-park, which slopes up to wooded ridges and contains an ornamental lake, haunt of ducks and waders; opposite lies the home park, traversed by a road that passes within sight of Moccas Court, then crosses the Wye by a private bridge offering pleasant river-views. Near the mansion is Moccas Church (45), a wholly early-Norman structure comprising apse, chancel and nave—a plain edition of the famous Kilpeck Church (p. 44). The

effigied de Freneye tomb (1330) in the chancel is worth studying. If you get or take leave to cross the bridge you come to
a noble avenue of Scotch firs called Monnington Walk—at
its farther end is the admirable Brobury Scar, a pine-fringed
cliff of red sandstone overlooking a sharp bend of the Wye—
and soon afterwards find yourself close to Monnington Court
and church. The latter was rebuilt (except the tower) in 1679
by Uvedall and Mary Tomkyns, who are commemorated by
grave-slabs in the chancel. The church is a favourable example
of its period, and contains interesting Carolean woodwork—
communion table and rails, screens, benches, gates (in tower
arch), doors, panelling and ornate pulpit. Notice the four-
gabled lychgate, cousin of that at Clun. The Court, originally
Elizabethan, was altered and extended by Uvedall Tomkyns,
but retains original panelling and plaster-work.

The supposed connexion of Owen Glyndwr with this
Monnington has been shown to be an error due to confusion
of similar names (see p. 28). A collateral relative of Uvedall
Tomkyns was Sir Uvedale Price, a product of Eton and Christ
Church, whose *Essay on the Picturesque*, published in 1794,
inaugurated a gentle revolt against the elaborate landscape-
gardening associated with the name of "Capability" Brown.
Price's estate of Foxley, five miles away on the slope of lovely
Ladylift Hill, was laid out on the "natural" lines he advocated,
though paradoxically the excellent results he achieved involved
far more labour and artistic skill than the creation of formal
gardens. On this topic one may point out that most of the
beauty of this Herefordshire countryside—as indeed much of
the rural beauty of all civilized countries—is due to the conscious planning and intelligent expenditure of artistically-
minded landowners. The pious sentiment of the drawing-
room ballad "God made the country, but Man made the town"
is a piece of muddle-headed cant. The country, as God made
it, was covered with vast impassable swamps, leagues of in-
tractable forest, barren mountains, bloated rivers and arid
deserts.[1]

Here I may digress to describe some places of interest.
Just where one of Wye's multitudinous loops approaches the
road quite closely, look up towards Mansell Hill and you
may discern Offa's Dyke, which crosses the hill longitudinally
and ceases abruptly at this river-loop. From this point southwards to below Monmouth, where the Dyke reappears on

[1] See on this theme T. Sharp's *Panorama of England* (published after the
above words were written).

the Gloucestershire bank near Redbrook, the Wye formed the Anglo-Cymric boundary.

Let us turn to right towards Hereford, and in one mile turn left, for Brinsop Court, which has more than one title to fame. First come a few cottages and, across a field, the *old* Brinsop church. Here is a good rood-screen, and the dragon-slaying George, patron saint of the church, is depicted both in the fourteenth-century glass of the east window and on a carved tympanum affixed to the north wall. Another chancel window commemorates the poet Wordsworth (see below). The building stands within low earthworks forming a square, perhaps an outwork for the protection of *Magna* (near Ken-chester), the Romano-British residential town on the road from *Viroconium* and *Bravonium* (Wroxeter and Leintwardine) to *Gobannium* and *Isca Silurum* (Abergavenny and Caerleon). We pass on between two detached, thickly wooded hills, and approach Brinsop Court across water-meadows wherein are

"Bulls that walk the pasture in kingly-flashing coats,"

each with his submissive harem of mild-eyed ruminant beeves: here the breeding of Herefordshires is carried on scientifically and on a large scale. Brinsop Court is a large moated manor-house, mainly Tudor, with a modernized interior, but retaining a Decorated chapel and hall. Passing the house you get a glimpse of symmetrical gables and a splendid cluster of chimneys; from a shaven lawn beyond a silvery pool rises a speading cedar tree, said to have been planted by William Wordsworth, a frequent visitor here during the tenancy of his brother-in-law; but—isn't the cedar rather large for its age?

If you continue forward you reach the direct road from Hereford to Weobley (p. 49); behind Nupton Hill, on the north, lies Buttas (p. 50), but there is no short-cut across the hill, though one may be shown on your map. So I shall imagine you transported back to Moccas.

Resuming the route for Hay from Moccas turning, one comes next to Bredwardine, where the traveller is advised first to make for the long and lofty bridge over the Wye, a structure of mellowed brick, a pleasant lounging place that offers perhaps the fairest river-views between Glasbury and Kerne Bridge. On the farther bank is a garden profuse with rhododendrons and other cultured plants; in the other direc-tion the view is bounded by the Knapp, a clump-crowned projection of Merbach Hill. Near the bridge, when the sun

37   THE HEREFORDSHIRE PLAIN FROM STOCKLEY HILL AT THE EDGE OF THE GOLDEN VALLEY

is genial, there are young people bathing and boating and village children paddling, all of them making a cheerful noise to the oldest god. Strolling back to the village, you see on your right the venerable Old Court, portions of which have stood for six centuries. On left is the parish church, of which the nave was built before 1100 and the chancel rebuilt in Edward I's reign, the two parts being therefore noticeably out of alignment. The village inn, more ancient than it looks, offers modern comforts: it sports the A.A. sign, and I have always found that the small or "one-star" A.A. hotels are pleasant places to stay in. Incidentally, the suffix in *Bredwardine* (cf. Leintwardine, Lugwardine) is simply another form of the more familiar "worthy" (as in Selworthy), and means "homestead" or "village clearing."

From Bredwardine the direct road to Hay first runs round the wooded flanks of Merbach Hill, passing, at New Weston Farm, a fine specimen of a *tallat* or open-sided barn, then after an undulating course in view of the Wye joins the road from Dorstone. For an alternative, cross the bridge and join the lower Hereford-Hay road at Letton, where the church has three features that deserve special notice: a timber-framed tower, placed on the north side; a Norman south doorway, with carved lintel and original door *in situ*; and a truly magnificent carved timber pulpit with enriched sounding-board, probably of the Queen-Anne period; a strange object to find in a remote village church. That brave warrior and fearlessly outspoken Lollard, Sir John Oldcastle, whom Henry V treated with such mean and cowardly ingratitude, held some property in Letton, though his seat was at Almeley, near Eardisley.

Nearing Whitney look out for the sign of the Stowe Inn, an old-fashioned homely place much frequented by hikers and cycling parties: it offers *and provides* clean and cheap accommodation and wholesome meals; and the bar-parlour is a resort of village worthies from whose lips you may hear much wisdom. At Whitney you approach the river: the village with its rebuilt church (the old church and Court were damaged by a flood) lies away on the right, and high above the village stands the modern Whitney Court, too opulent-looking; on the left is the Boat Inn, more sophisticated than the "Stowe," and offering bathing and boating facilities, as the river runs immediately behind it. Since Hay is—only just—in Wales, the "Boat" is thronged on Sabbath evenings with thirsty burgesses of Hay and the more emancipated of their women-folk. Beyond this Bacchic refuge from a man-made desert the road runs between strips of plantation that in due season display the rich and varied colours of rhododendron blooms. Emerging from these floral walls we reach a parting of the ways where the Wye is crossed by an old toll-bridge of timber.

The branch (A438) that crosses Whitney bridge is the main road to Hay and Brecon: the nearer, left-bank road (B4350) proceeds by way of Clyro to Glasbury, where it crosses the Wye and joins A438. For the present let us stick to the less frequented left-bank road, which offers the more charming glimpses of the winding river and the more satisfying views of the Black Mountains escarpment. Beyond the fork our road is soon joined by the steep lane descending from Brilley (p. 66); then comes Rhydspence Inn, the "last House in England" (*house* being used in the esoteric, Dionysiac sense). Opposite the inn is a notice-board the wording of which suggests that this was a "house" habitually "used" by the early Lords Marchers or the retinue of Llewelyn ap Gruffydd. But the disillusioned savants of the Historical Monuments Commission assign it to the Tudor period.

A few yards beyond Rhydspence we cross the border and enter Radnorshire. Above on the right, the ground rises rapidly to the outer heights of the tangle of hills that lies between the Wye and Radnor Vale. On the left the river recedes to flow under the scarp crowned by the scanty ruins of Clifford Castle; then again approaches the road, and near Clyro again recedes, looping round the site of a small Roman fort. Clyro is a pleasant village with a most efficiently conducted country-house-like inn, the Baskerville Arms. Hay is reached from Clyro by a road which, after a long up-and-down mile, crosses the Wye by a lofty iron bridge. Just outside the village on the left of the Hay road is a tree-clad knoll concealing a motte-and-bailey — all that remains of Clyro Castle. This lordship was in the de Braose territories, but was later (and until quite recently) held by the Baskervilles.

Continuing westwards by the Glasbury road, you at once pass an embattled gateway admitting to a farmyard. This is a relic of Old Clyro Court, once the home of the Bredwardine Vaughans; presently the modern Clyro Court, the replica of a lovely Elizabethan mansion destroyed by fire, is seen in a spacious park on right. The destroyed mansion was built by some Baskerville who wearied of the discomfort of the old

9 THE SOUTH DOOR, KILPECK, WITH ELABORATE CELTIC CARVING

41 NEARLY SIX CENTURIES AFTER: THE 18TH
CENTURY APSE OF CARVED WOOD REREDOS OF

40 THE NORMAN INTERIOR OF KILPECK CHURCH

stone castle. Beyond Llowes, the next village, road and river approach each other, and across the valley Lord Hereford's Knob looks truly knob-like. A pretty dingle is crossed, then a steep lane comes in from the right, skirting a vast park. The lane leads to the little old Nonconformist chapel of Maesyronnen, which retains the arrangement and much furniture of the Commonwealth period. The park is that of Maesllwch Castle, a vast pseudo-Gothic pile, complete with multiplicity of towers and battlemented walls, with arrow-slits and mullioned casements opening on a shocked countryside, and for all I know with barbican, portcullis and drawbridge. It suggests the American film-producer's dream of a rich man's rural home. This Victorian petrification of the spirit of plutocracy was erected in the mid-nineteenth century for a de Winton, head of a family which emigrated from Holland in the seventeenth century.

Skirting the park, our road approaches Glasbury, a large scattered village, which occupies both banks of the Wye, being thus in two counties: the ugly modern-Gothic church is on the Brecon bank, and the two parts are linked by a graceful bridge from which in clear weather one obtains an impressive distant view of the Brecon Beacons. The bridge, a favourite promenading place of the younger village folk, brings us into the main Hay-Brecon highway. The road we have just left continues westwards—much rougher now—as a winding, hilly lane to Boughrood, beyond which one may follow it past Llanstephan, the mouth of the Bach Howey glen and Aberedw to Llanelwedd near Builth; but for a less distracted enjoyment of the superlative beauties of the Wye gorge between Llyswen and Builth—a stretch of the river far more delightful than the charabangers' "Wye Valley"—it is best to cross Boughrood Bridge and join the main Brecon-Builth highway.

Let us now return to the toll-house of Whitney Bridge, cross that curious old structure—which recalls prints of the old Putney Bridge—and follow the road along the southern bank. This rises gradually to Clifford, where the remains of the castle are approached by a cart-track on right: when you reach them, step carefully to avoid sudden holes and chunks of masonry concealed by brambles and nettles. Quite recently, within what was a subsidiary bailey, a desirable villa residence of pink brick has been erected close to these crumbling walls! The masonry remains of the castle are of Edwardian date, but may occupy the site of an earlier motte-and-bailey constructed

F

by William FitzOsborn, Earl of Hereford.[1] This became the castle of a Lordship Marcher and passed by marriage to a knight who took the surname of de Clifford. One of the later de Cliffords, Walter, was the father of the "Fair Rosamund," Henry II's mistress, and of Roger, who married his ward, the heiress of the Viponts, and thus became master of vast estates in and about the northern Pennines. After his time the Clifford lordship passed to the Mortimers. Antiquarians should struggle up the hill separating the village from the church, which contains a thirteenth-century effigy, carved in timber, of a priest in mass vestments.

The approach to Hay is a long gentle downhill bordered on left by the undulating park of The Moor. The town itself is placed on an eminence, so that the entries from both this and the Brecon side are fairly steep ascents; on the north there is an abrupt drop to the Wye, here a broad and shallow stream crossed by the bridge that carries the road to Clyro; immediately to south rise the foothills of the Black Mountains; for various reasons it is difficult to get a satisfactory view of the town as a whole. Its buildings, a not unpleasing medley of the picturesque, the stolidly respectable, and the purely utilitarian, have as focus Hay Castle, which consists of a handsome Jacobean house linked to remnants—a gateway and tower—of a Norman castle. It is the market for a wide district and on market days is full of life and colour; during these weekly feasts the inquiring stranger can get plenty of local colour by visiting the bar of the "Crown."

Towards the west end of the town, overlooking the river, is the parish church, rebuilt (except for its fortress-like tower) during last century in an appalling variety of the "churchwarden" style. The strangest feature is a quasi-Moorish arcade separating nave from chancel. Between the church and the town is the original Hay Castle, a large motte of bold outline. The Norman castle was built in Henry I's reign by a knight named Revell, who also endowed the church, and rebuilt in John's reign by William de Braose or—according to local legend—by his wife, the "shrewd, malapert and stomachful" Maud de Valérie, who as "Maud Walbee," was credited with superhuman powers. She certainly had good store of courage: she accused King John to his face of murdering his nephew Arthur; for which tactlessness she was immured in Corfe Castle and starved to death. Meanwhile William de Braose

---

[1] Some authorities identify FitzOsborn's motte with Newton Tump, near Dorstone.

42 WHITE CASTLE, MONMOUTHSHIRE, FROM ITS MOAT

43 THE ENTRANCE TOWERS, RAGLAN CASTLE, MONMOUTHSHIRE
CASTLE CONTRASTS: DEFENSIVE AND RESIDENTIAL

44 SKENFRITH CHURCH, MONMOUTHSHIRE, WITH TYPICAL
BORDER BELFRY

45 THE NORMAN CHURCH OF MOCCAS ON THE WYE

had fled to France, a typical piece of poltroonery. He was, in modern parlance, a nasty bit of work. Cunning, greedy, treacherous, cowardly and ostentatiously pious, he was the only Lord Marcher who can fairly be called an unmitigated blackguard. In brief periods of peace and under a just lord the varied populace of Hay lived in harmony, the town being divided into "Welsh Hay" and "English Hay." The present English-Welsh boundary is the Dulas brook, which forms the delightful Cusop Dingle and trickles into the Wye near the railway station. The opposite bank of the river belongs to Radnorshire.

The main or lower Hay-Talgarth road offers many alluring glimpses of the Black Mountains escarpment and almost continuous views of the winding Wye. Some four miles from Hay, after Glasbury, comes a gentle slope terminating at the almost historic Three Cocks Inn: the inn-sign, three gilt cocks in relief on a background of powder-blue, assures the questing wayfarer that this is no commonplace hostelry. It is a house of some antiquity, and within it you find such old-fashioned features as stair-gates and doors that have latches worked by bobbins. For some generations it was in the hands of the same family and was the rendezvous of sportsmen of the old school, especially anglers: A. G. Bradley has given a charming description of that *ancien régime* in his *Highways and Byways in South Wales*.

From the "Three Cocks" the road ascends through the hamlet of Aberllyfni, passing successively the turning for Builth, the gates of Gwerynfed Park, a finely-timbered demesne, and the short approach to Three Cocks Junction, draughty meeting-place of lines from Hereford, Brecon and Builth. At the next road-fork bear left for Talgarth. Presently the castellated mansion of Porthamel, now a farmhouse, is seen on right, and on left the massive tower of Talgarth Church appears against a background formed by the pyramidal Mynydd Troed (p. 13). The main Brecon road is reached from Talgarth by a short cross-road which passes close to Bronllys Castle, a massive and lofty round keep built in the first part of the fourteenth century, and still in good preservation. The road to Brecon, comparatively unexciting for the first few miles, offers later a succession of glorious views of the Brecon Beacons seen across the Usk Valley, and approaches Brecon by a descent alongside a magnificent wooded gorge watered by the greater Honddu. The upper Hay-Talgarth road, which leaves the lower road a mile from Hay, is useful for those wishing to attack the Black Mountains escarpment by less obvious routes; there are troublesome tracks, hard to trace but practicable, from Llanigon and Velindre.

.   .   .   .

Before faring south to explore the middle Monnow valley let us look at two remarkable ancient buildings: Kilpeck Church and White Castle. Kilpeck is not far from the foot of the Golden Valley, but the simplest approach is by either of two turnings marked "To St. Devereux[1] Station" which leave the Hereford-Abergavenny highway four miles north of Pontrilas; after crossing the railway turn left; the churchway starts opposite the inn. A church built here before the Conquest is now represented by the north-east external angle of the nave, where notice the "Saxon" quoins. William I granted the manor to his friend William FitzNorman, whose son Hugh built a stone castle to west of the church; of the castle only earthworks and two fragments of a polygonal keep remain (38). The present church was built in the period 1150–75: it is perhaps the most remarkable example of enriched late-Romanesque work in the country; experts trace Scandinavian influence in details of the profuse ornamentation. In plan it consists of nave, chancel and apsidal sanctuary (p. 9), with a narrow west bay: the building has a western bell-cote (modern) and a south doorway. Externally, each part of the building has pilaster buttresses, and corbel-tables resting on corbels (38), eighty-six in all, carved with an amazing variety of subjects; among them, for instance, may be mentioned a beak-head with a human figure in its jaws, pig's head, bull's head, monkey, dancing figure in kilt, grotesque playing rebeck, birds biting snake, hawk and bird, grotesque figures embracing, and a quite pagan "fertility" figure. The famous south doorway (39) has a tympanum carved with a conventionalized vine-spray, and an outer arch showing beak-heads of various patterns, some unique; in place of a dripstone is an outer row of medallions carved with grotesques; the western jamb-shaft is carved with two figures of warriors in Phrygian caps, ribbed hauberks and *bracae* or trews, singularly resembling rather long plus fours, held up by elaborately knotted scarves. It is believed that these represent the much-feared wild Welshmen.

Internally, the church is divided into its three portions by Norman arches: the chancel arch is heavily enriched (40). Noteworthy features are the vaulting of the apse, the respond

[1] "St. Devereux" is the Welsh saint Dyfrig (Dubricius); not a connexion of the present Lord Hereford.

shafts of the chancel arch (each is formed by three carved figures of apostles wearing *nimbi* and strained expressions: a key identifies St. Peter), the seventeenth-century balustraded west gallery, and—preserved in the apse—the Norman stoup, carved round the bowl with a pair of clutching hands.

Now for White Castle: any one paying a first visit by car should approach the castle from the south, that is, by the lane leading north from Llantilio Crossenny, a village on the Monmouth-Abergavenny highway. The special excellence of White Castle as a "sight" is its marvellous state of preservation: the walls and towers of the main portion, though the towers are roofless, are otherwise almost intact; so that from outside it looks pretty well the same as it looked more than six centuries ago (42). The turrets and breached wall of the barbican, which with earthworks on the south constituted the outer line of defence, will be of interest to antiquarians. The castle proper consists of curtain walls of great thickness built round an inner court to form a hexagon, with a massive round tower at each angle: the north side is much shorter than the rest, so that here there are two towers fairly close together: between them is the main entrance. Unlike the other two castles of the Trilateral (p. 35), Grosmont and Skenfrith, White Castle was never used as a residence: it was purely military, its garrisons being accommodated probably in penthouses ranged along the inner faces of the walls. When once more you find yourself outside the outer wall, walk a little westward along a grassy track and half-way down a sloping meadow; then look back at the walls and towers, now partly hidden by the crest of the slope. This, to one endowed with imagination, will be a strange and thrilling experience; for a few moments consciousness of the time-dimension will be lost. The same spot may be reached on foot from Llanvetherine, on the Abergavenny-Ross road, by way of the little Trothy valley: this route is for walkers the most romantic approach.

The various points of interest in and about the Monnow valley will for convenience be embraced in the description of a single circular trip, Pontrilas being taken as the starting-point. From Pontrilas follow the main road south for two miles, then take the Grosmont turn. Grosmont, now a quiet village, only ceased to be a borough in 1860. The size of the church and its ambitious planning—it is cruciform, with transepts, aisles and a south chancel chapel—attest the importance of the mediæval town. Noteworthy features of the church are the octagonal tower with its spire, the massive but unfinished nave arcade, and the handsome south chapel.

Grosmont Castle, the most elaborate unit of the Trilateral, included a banqueting-hall: the much-photographed chimney is a relic of this. Otherwise the ruins comprise only remnants of the inner ward gateway, the keep and one curtain wall with two drum towers, all dating from a rebuilding by John or Henry III. The Border lords shared the disgust aroused in the English barons by Henry III's preference of foreign favourites, and some of them allied themselves with Llewelyn the Great, whose activities caused the king to garrison Grosmont, with himself personally in charge. Llewelyn with Welsh and Border troops made a surprise night attack and drove the defenders out in hopeless confusion: the foreign officers had donned their nightshirts, and had to run away in these effeminate garments. The south chapel of the church is said to have been built at the charges of Henry's consort, Eleanor of Provence: may we suppose that she too was present on this humiliating occasion, and had to make a flight through the bramble bushes and over nasty jagged stones in a flimsy *robe-de-nuit*? An event of more serious importance was the defeat here 170 years later of Owen Glyndwr's lieutenant, Rhys Gethin, by Harry of Monmouth (not yet Henry V). After this disaster Glyndwr's star soon faded into obscurity.

On this side of the Monnow we are in Herefordshire; the opposite bank is in Monmouthshire. We pass down the valley, skirting Garway Hill; beyond the opposite bank rises another massive height, Graig Serrerthin. (Walkers who require short cuts will find useful tracks, which also offer fine panoramas, crossing both these hills.) Garway Hill was once the chase or private hunting-ground of the Knights Hospitallers of Garway, which soon comes into view a little below the road; a village that wears an Arcadian air (48), though it is not far from Skenfrith, and must once have known stirring times. The church, which gives an impression of hoar antiquity, was held in succession by Knights Templars and Knights Hospitallers: the former built the chancel and—as elsewhere—a *round* nave, of which foundations have been unearthed; the present nave with its south chapel, and the keep-like tower, which stands obliquely to the nave and is linked to it by a low stone corridor, are ascribed to the Hospitallers, who also erected the great *columbarium* or dovecot seen among neighbouring farm buildings. Interesting

46 THE WYE VALLEY AT BREDWARDINE

47 FARM RANGES NEAR CLYRO, IN THE WYE VALLEY

8. GARWAY BY THE MONNOW, SHOWING THE DETACHED FORTRESS-LIKE TOWER OF THE CHURCH

features of the church are the elaborate Norman chancel arch, the exposed rood-loft stairs, the large dug-out chest in the chapel, primitive oak benches in the nave, and amateurish sky-and-stars decoration of walls and roof. The dovecot, circular, stone-roofed and vaulted, contained 666 pigeon-holes.

Passing St. Weonards, with the fortified mansion of Treago, and Welsh Newton, at the Broad Oak cross-roads we turn left along A40 and soon recross the Monnow and enter Skenfrith close to the castle, which is simple in plan: a quadrilateral of high curtain walls, with drum-towers at the angles, enclosing a court in which stands a high circular keep. Up the village street you see the massive church tower, which like several others in the district has a timber-framed upper stage (44). Skenfrith is a favourite angler's resort, the Monnow being much esteemed for its trout fishing. For the remainder of the route you can either follow A40 to Abergavenny or branch off northwards in a few miles, at Cross Ash, and follow a lane that skirts the southern end of Graig Serrerthin and runs along the high ridge of Campstone hill, finally de-livering you at Pandy. If you choose the Abergavenny road, look out for Llanvetherine Church, on the chancel wall of which is a slab carved in relief with the portrait of a Welsh lady wearing the high-crowned beaver proper to her period (1775). Near the second milestone from Abergavenny a stile gives access to a path that ascends, at first through a wood, to the bare razor-edge leading to the summit of Skyrrid Fawr, whence you may enjoy an almost "close-up" view of the Sugar-Loaf and the ends of the Black Mountains ridges, and examine the great notch—the result of a landslide—that gives this fine isolated height its distinctive appearance. In the Middle Ages the natives had installed into them a belief that vibrations of the earthquake consequent upon the Crucifixion had travelled all the way to Monmouthshire: Skyrrid's riven crest was for them a Divine sign. Much more commonly it is the Devil that is credited with odd or startling natural features.

For Abergavenny and the Sugar-Loaf, see Chapter X.

CHAPTER V

NORTH HEREFORDSHIRE: ITS VILLAGES OF HALF-TIMBERED BUILDINGS

HEREFORDSHIRE, Shropshire and Cheshire are the counties that contain the greatest number and variety and the finest examples of timber-framed buildings, both dwellings and other structures such as market halls and dovecots. From Shropshire the style overflows into the adjacent parts of Montgomeryshire and Radnorshire. In Herefordshire students and admirers of half-timbered buildings will find ample material within the Trilateral defined by the points Hereford, Kington and Richard's Castle (near Ludlow). Hereford itself and Leominster possess certain notable examples, but only a thorough search will reveal how large a number of such buildings they retain: in any largish town of continuous organic growth these relics of a more leisurely and less luxurious age tend to be sacrificed to the spirit of *fin de siècle*. Ledbury, with its Market House, Feathers Inn, Biddulph mansion and almost incredible Church Lane, is outside the province of this book.

To savour this building style to the full you must seek out and contemplate either superb isolated examples such as the Ley near Weobley (60), or Buttas near King's Pyon (50), or whole villages or little towns of half-timbered structures. Within the limits defined above are Weobley (52) and Pembridge (9, 58), Eardisland (59, 61, 63), Orleton and Yarpole; of these five townlets and villages the main portions consist almost wholly of such buildings, and these not only show great diversity of pattern—squares, circles, trefoils and quatrefoils as well as vertical and horizontal striping and "herring-bone" —but are, many of them, embellished with elaborate carving on corner-posts, beams, brackets and gable-end barge-boards, with "pargeting" or figured plaster-work and, structurally, with dormer-windows, cupolas, porches and balustraded balconies. Primitive specimens, again, are seen in remote little villages like Adforton (81) or Leinthall Earls (p. 75).

The places of which descriptions now follow will be found to comprise between them a large proportion of the county's

49   THE TOWER OF HEREFORD CATHEDRAL FROM THE WYE

"black-and-white" buildings.[1] In Sarnesfield churchyard, beyond the cross-roads, is the tomb of one whose memory admirers of prime half-timbered work should surely bless: John Abel (1577–1674) the "King's Carpenter," or rather "Architector" as he calls himself in the curiously donnish epitaph: its closing lines:

> " His house of clay could hold no longer;
> May Heaven's joy frame him a stronger "

may glance at the primitive daub-and timber fashion which he improved into a mode of beauty.

Weobley, a mile south of the main road, is approached by the next turning. Its three main streets and their tributaries contain few buildings that do not flaunt the magpie colours. Among the most delightful are the Old School House, Throne Farm opposite, and the "Red Lion" at the corner of the lane leading to the church (52). The latter, except for the south aisle and doorway, is of the Decorated period. The slender spire crowns a perfectly-proportioned but windowless tower placed at the end of the north aisle.

Of Weobley Castle little remains but earthworks on the south side of the town. Within easy reach of Weobley are three examples of half-timbered work—The Ley, Fenhampton and Buttas—that "should on no account be missed": the phrase is not here an exaggeration. The first two lie off the main Hereford road (B4230): The Ley, approached by a gated turning to right just outside the town, is a spacious Elizabethan mansion with walls of rich red framed in timbers faded to grey (60). The front of the house shows no less than eight gables, for below two gable-ends are other gables that shield projecting windows, and there is a projecting porch with a gabled upper storey. The initials I. B. over the porch refer to James Bridges, who inherited the property from his ancestors, de Brugges of Bridge Sollers. The Ley should also be viewed from the farther bank of the pool that represents the moat (60). Returning to the road, proceed along it till well beyond the imposing entrance-gates of the Garnstone demesne; you will then see, on right, the long two-storied black-and-white frontage of Fenhampton, amid a setting of trim orchard and pasture. Both Fenhampton and The Ley are noted for the breeding and rearing of Herefordshire cattle.

---

[1] Or "black-and-red." In the larger houses the filling of the timber frames is sometimes red brick or sandstone: in cottages clay or the primitive daub is often used, and the filling, of whatever material, is as a rule whitewashed.

Buttas should, by those capable of æsthetic thrills, be first approached from the Weobley direction. Passing over the flank of Buttas Knapp, whence on clear days you can look through gaps between sylvan eminences to the Clee Hills northwards, eastwards to the Malverns, you suddenly come into sight of a delightful old farmhouse, red brick in timber framing. This is Buttas[1]: close by stands the oft-photographed "dovecot" (50), actually a falconry, consisting of a gateway of which the upper storey was used for homing pigeons or mewed falcons. The barge-boards and brackets are richly carved, and in one panel is the date of erection, 1632. The massed woods of Nupton Hill make a sumptuous background.

Let us now return to Weobley, rejoin the main road and turn again in the direction of Leominster. Dilwyn, the next village, is dominated by its church, which occupies a knoll above the road. A meagre timber spire forms an anticlimax to the massive tower and tall clerestory windows. The usual entrance is through an unusually fine porch of the Decorated period. The chancel-screen is much admired, but the tracery and coving are modern, though their beauty cannot be denied. The village seems to suffer unduly from the enterprise of travelling billposters. Two cross-roads are passed before Monkland is reached: the first gives access to Pembridge and Eardisland (pp. 52, 53), the second to Kingsland. Monkland got its name from an alien priory founded here in William II's reign. Leominster would be the natural finale of this trip: Luston, however, lies only three miles north of Leominster on the western (B4361) of the two direct Ludlow roads. Luston is a single long street of houses and cottages most of which are at least two hundred and fifty years old (62).

Leominster—pronounced not B.B.C. fashion but as it appears on old milestones, *Lemster*—retains many timber-framed houses: good specimens may be seen in Drapers' Row and Bridge Street, but the stranger is advised to saunter about and make discoveries for himself; he will also find jolly street-names like Bargates and Fosbury. The town seems first to have grown up round a Benedictine nunnery founded by Godiva, famous wife of that earl of Mercia whose name appears abbreviated in the early form of the town's name— Leofminstre. After the Conquest the nunnery became a monastery, and Norman monastic buildings arose, including a noble church with central tower and two aisles. The town population increased in numbers and wealth, until the burghers

[1] "Butthouse" is a pedagogic miscorrection.

52   AFTER A SHARP SHOWER AT WEOBLEY

53   LEOMINSTER PRIORY CHURCH: THE EAST END, WITH BALLFLOWER-ENCRUSTED
WINDOWS IN THE SOUTH AISLE

began to demand a proper *parish* church, where they should not be relegated to the end of an aisle. There was a compromise: the Norman nave and north aisle remained as the minster church; the old south aisle was demolished and a new nave and south aisle in the Early English style erected to serve as the parish church. In the Decorated period the south aisle windows were replaced by others profusely adorned with the typical "ball-flower" (53). The Perpendicular west tower was added when the central tower was taken down for safety: why Tudor dormer-windows were substituted for Norman windows in the north aisle, nobody knows. Unhappily the east end of the church was totally destroyed by fire in 1699, and has not been rebuilt. The domestic buildings, too, have disappeared. The large, elaborate ducking-stool (p. 62)—a "super" one, surely—displayed in the north aisle attracts many women sightseers: they come in pairs or bevies, whisper, giggle and—walk out unconscious that there is anything else worth seeing.

During the Stuart period Leominster attained great commercial eminence: it was renowned for its wheaten flour and fine manchet bread, but above all, for its wool shorn from the backs of Ryelands sheep, which brought in so much good money—the

> "Lemster ore
> That with the silkworm's web for fineness doth compare;"

so old Drayton boasts.

Not far from the church, at one end of a small but pretty cricket ground, stands the celebrated Grange House, built in 1633 by John Abel. This was once the "Butter Cross" or Market Hall and stood near the town centre: less than eighty years ago the sordid vandals who then composed the town council proposed to demolish it, but it was bought—for £95 —by a neighbouring landowner, carefully transported to its present position, and for a time used as a residence. It has lost its dormer windows but acquired a cupola. This is a truly splendid example of half-timbered construction: the lower storey has exterior arcading, the upper storey oriel windows resting on balustrades; overhanging gables crown the whole (51). The outer beams supporting the upper floor are carved with a continuous inscription in a queer "Macaronic" jumble of Latin and English. Brackets, spandrels and principal beams are richly carved with figures as well as conventional patterns.

Pembridge and Eardisland are so delightful that no mere cursory "once-over" will so much as skim the cream of their beauties. Pembridge should be approached from the south, so as to enter the main street at a point where you are close to the three principal "sights": the church, the primitive-looking Market Hall, and the venerable New Inn (9). The pleasing irregularity of the inn's exterior reflects the rambling waywardness of rooms and passages within. The Mortimers procured market rights for the little town, but no longer are markets or hiring fairs held here: the open Market Hall, formed by eight stout pillars of timber supporting a broad roof, is now but a shelter from rain and a place for smoking and salivatory rumination. The churchyard is gained by a long flight of steps: the detached fourteenth-century belfry at once claims attention (58). This consists of a roomy octagon of stone with deep pyramidal roof, surmounted by a much smaller square stage of timber, weather-boarded and louvred, from the roof of which rises the similar but smaller final stage. The three roofs are of stone tiles: peer inside the doorway if unlocked to see how the upper stages are supported on ancient rough-hewn tree trunks. The belfry faintly resembles a pagoda, but narrows more suddenly. The church, which is of the Decorated period, reflects the former importance of the little town, having transepts, aisles and clerestoried nave; in the chancel is a great tomb supporting a strange assortment of effigies. A leisurely stroll through Pembridge's few streets will display typical "magpie" houses and cottages in great variety.

Eardisland (63) is a Kate Greenaway village, a thing of perfect joy. Its superior charm need not be closely analysed: one factor may be the way the buildings are spaced out, straggling in careless irregularity along the road's broad green borders; another is certainly the presence of the ubiquitous Arrow, which passes under a bridge near one end of the village. Beyond the bridge, on the left bank of the stream, is a lovely half-timbered mansion (61), two-storied, with ancient moss-grown roof of stone: men call it the Old Vicarage, but guide-books Staick House. Its delightful gardens, cheerful with blends of brilliant colours and watered by the silvery Arrow, are separated from it by the road (63). The bridge-approach has on one side a rambling black-and-white house, on the other, a cupolaed Tudor dovecot of red brick and greying timbers, whose four gables are wavily mirrored in the stream. Two inns standing back from the road provide sound

ale and homely fare served with simple kindliness: ducks in
the river quack an *obbligato* to your munchings and swallow-
ings, and now and then a cow moos gently from the inn
paddock.

By leaving the village in the direction of Leominster and
taking the first lane to left you will soon reach Kingsland,
entering it at right angles to a main street pleasantly bordered
by "magpie" houses interspersed with more ambitious dwellings; a tall pine-tree lends distinction to one of the gardens.
The church, said to have been built about 1300 by one of the
Mortimers, who bestowed the living on an unwarlike son, is
chiefly noted for its "Volca" (or Volker?) chamber, which
fills the angle between the east wall of the north porch and the
north wall of the church (p. 34). This was probably a chantry
chapel, and its hollowed recess may have contained an effigy;
an "Easter Sepulchre" would hardly have been placed so far
from the main altar, and before its windows were glazed this
chamber would have been too draughty to accommodate the
most ascetic anchorite.

From Kingsland take the lane running north, and after
crossing a bridge over the Lugg turn right, by a road that
follows the course of the river. The journey may end at
Leominster (p. 50), but if the traveller wants to push on to
Ludlow, let him choose the eastern (A49) of the two direct
roads. Let him also, after skirting the spacious park of Berring-
ton Hall, and before approaching Brimfield, look out for a
lane on right which will bring him to the marvellous old
mansion of Nun Upton (he must bear right at first fork and
turn left at next road-junction). At Eye, by the station, the
austere severity of the manor house leaves one unprepared for
the splendid series of richly modelled high-relief plaster
ceilings of the late seventeenth century. One may complete
the detour by way of Little Hereford (p. 55), rejoining the
main road at Woofferton (p. 55). For Ludlow, see pp. 73, 78.

Good black-and-white work is seen at Eardisley and Kington (see Chapter VI), and in richer variety at Yarpole and
Orleton, villages little inferior to Weobley and Pembridge. In
a secluded situation is an almost perfect Queen-Anne house,
red brick with stone facings, bearing the impressive title
Court of Noke (54). More than one tenant of this mansion and
its wide farm-lands has contributed towards the improvement
of the Herefordshire breed of cattle. The stream you cross
by Noke Bridge is the Arrow, which has come all the way
from the wilds above Gladestry and now flows on towards

Pembridge and Eardisland, to join the Lugg below Leominster. At the lower end of Shobdon stands a half-timbered inn, a handsome though not ancient example of the style. On left are the drive-gates of Shobdon Court. Walk up this drive past the site of the demolished Renaissance house, then along a field-path till you reach some remains—chancel arch and two doorways with tympana—of a ruined church. These were set up here in the Jane-Austen Age, when it was fashionable to have ruins in your park; they are contemporary with Kilpeck Church, and the carvings on two of the shafts include similar Cymric warriors (five on each shaft) wearing similar trews (see p. 44); but long exposure has blunted much fine detail.

A carfax is reached at Mortimer's Cross, scene of the battle which placed Edward IV on the throne. An obelisk here bears an appropriate inscription. The battle, in which the Yorkists under the young Edward severely defeated a Lancastrian force under Jasper Tudor, Earl of Pembroke, took place mainly between the south-east angle of the cross-roads and the Lugg bank. The bulk of the forces on both sides were Welshmen or men of the Marches; for both Jasper and Edward's second-in-command, William Herbert, were of Welsh descent, and Edward himself had the blood of the ancient Welsh princes in his veins. One of the captured in this fight was Jasper's father, Owen, who was at once conveyed to Hereford for execution: soon the headsman's bloody axe struck off that still comely head which a queen's lily-white hands had oft caressed. For this was that Owen Tudor whom for love of his *beaux yeux* Katharine, widow (and previously grass-widow) of Henry V, had insisted on marrying; a marriage that brought the descendants of petty Anglesey squires—not, as they pretended, of Welsh Princes—into the sacred rank of royalty.

Facing north at Mortimer's Cross, the right-hand road leads to Leominster, but the forward way is the Knighton road by way of Aymestrey and Wigmore, whence a way leads over Maryknowl at 900 ft. to Ludlow. At Adforton is joined the Ludlow-Knighton road which has come 800 ft. over Fiddler's Elbow and past Leintwardine. For the present let us trace an easier route that allows some interesting digressions. Crossing the Lugg bridge and continuing forward, we soon pass the aggressive red-brick buildings of Lucton School, founded in 1708 by one John Pierrepont, whose life-sized image, pallid rather than white, glares at nothing from above the portal. This is, however, a school held locally in much esteem. Looking south-eastwards from the next rise one enjoys a compre-

54 "COURT OF NOKE," BY THE ARROW, NEAR PEMBRIDGE

5 A HEREFORDSHIRE FARMHOUSE AT BLACKHALL, KING'S PYON

STRINGING HOPS FOR THE NEW

A HEREFORDSHIRE ORCHARD AT

hensive landscape that vividly recalls some of the master-pieces of Claude Lorrain and Nicolas Poussin. On the Welsh side the Black Mountains appear as far-away clouds. Soon we skirt a wide park graced by massive oaks and Spanish chest-nuts, through which are seen the towers and battlements of the much-restored Croft Castle, and beside it a little ancient church with a foreign-looking bell-cupola.

Paths across the farther end of the park climb to lovely Bircher Common and the bold height of Croft Ambrey with its great camp and incomparable views; from our road a right-hand lane rises and dips to Yarpole, whose two streets, meet-ing in a wide angle, are chequered with Tudor houses and cottages. The church has a detached steeple bearing a general resemblance to that of Pembridge but simpler and smaller. Beyond the park of Bircher Court and ensuing cross-roads we emerge into the Leominster-Ludlow highway at a point whence there is a most satisfying view of Bircher Common—it appears as an inverted green bowl dotted thickly with the brilliant yellow of gorse-bushes and bordered below with a broad belt of more delicate green—a plantation of young larches. Hence proceed towards Ludlow till you reach the Maidenhead Inn (on left) which offers modest comfort to visitors: the turning opposite leads up to Orleton, another village almost wholly composed of black-and-white buildings set at a great diversity of angles: the loveliest, which shows many gables and a projecting porch with rooms above it, is Orleton Court, long the property of the Blounts, but devised by the eccentric will of the last of them, an aggrieved Roman Catholic and *laudator temporis acti*, to the ultra-modern and mostly Protestant Yale University! The Peggy Blount with whom the poet Pope philandered was one of the Orleton Blounts; and the village was the birthplace of Adam de Orleton, Bishop of Hereford, who was an intimate counsellor of Edward II's queen and contrived her paramour Roger Mortimer's escape from the Tower, yet after Edward III had avenged his father's murder managed to retain royal favour. The road through the village comes into the Woofferton road at the hamlet of Comberton, where notice two or three barns of uncommon construction—the walls are of thin laths closely plaited, so as to resemble basket-work. The Salwey Arms at Woofferton is recommended as a very satisfactory feeding-place, but first it is worth while to follow the Tenbury road as far as Little Hereford, where there are half-timbered houses large and small, ancient and modernized, grouped round a church with a keep-like tower. Northwards from the village across the valley of the Ledwyche Brook Titterstone Clee looms massively: to north-west, as you return to Woofferton, the sparkle of the Teme guides the eye towards High Vinnalls and Bringewood Chase.

From Woofferton a broad highway runs direct to Ludlow; a more interesting, hillier route leads onward from the inn near Orleton mentioned above, passing through the half-timbered village of Richard's Castle. Both the earthworks and the masonry ruins here are important in the history of castle development. The original Richard was Richard Fitz-Scrob, a Norman on whom Edward the Confessor bestowed land in this district. The earthworks, a high flattened mound with a basecourt surrounded by a moat, are a perfect example of a Saxon burh; of the masonry castle portions of the keep and curtain walls remain: if these were built by Richard (which is hardly credible) the castle was the earliest Norman fortress of stone in the country. Ludlow is approached through its delightful old Teme-side neighbour Ludford (p. 79).

In Hereford itself the magpie livery must be sought in the humbler streets. Abel's vast and splendid half-timber town hall has been swept away by soulless city fathers and now lives only in Clayton's plates, but one splendid black-and-white building remains at the city's centre—the Old House, perhaps John Abel's masterpiece. Here now is the Hereford Museum, which contains numerous finds unearthed at Kenchester (p. 38). A topographical tour of the city should include Garrick's birthplace and Coningsby Hospital (both in Wide-marsh Street; the Coningsby "servitors"—alas!—are no longer garbed in their period livery); the preaching cross, relic of a demolished friary, behind the Hospital; the stalls and misericords of St. Peter's and All Saints', and the chained library of the latter church; the castle grounds, and the fifteenth-century Wye Bridge.

For several centuries Hereford Castle was a storm centre, for Hereford was involved not only in constant Border warfare but in every outbreak of civil strife from the time of Stephen to that of Cromwell. In Leland's day the oft-rebuilt castle, though tending towards ruin, had walls still "high and strong and full of great Toures." In the Great Rebellion it was re-paired and held by Royalist forces, but finally taken by Colonel Birch of Weobley, after which it was wholly demolished. Fragments of the mediæval city walls remain here and there (*e.g.* in Wall Street), but the six gates have vanished.

58   THE DETACHED BELFRY OF PEMBRIDGE CHURCH

60 THE LEY FARMHOUSE, WEOBLEY

61 STAICK HOUSE, EARDISLAND

And now the Cathedral. No detailed description can be given here, but a few impressions may be recorded, a few suggestions made. This splendid pile of stone, embodying work of all the four great periods (and, very unfortunately, of the neo-Gothic period too), is the ultimate development of a shrine built over the bones of Aethelberht, King of Kent, by the great Mercian King, Offa. Poor Offa has incurred unmerited obloquy for a natural action due to his manhood. Aethelberht had come to these parts to pay his addresses to Offa's daughter: at a banquet he met the mother, Offa's consort, and was smitten with a violent fancy for her; later, he pestered her; she complained; Offa gave his bodyguard certain orders; when next Aethelberht made amorous approach to Offa's queen, his head was struck off. This act of rude justice was seized upon by the Church as a fine opportunity for propaganda; Aethelberht, you see, was a Christian, Offa a pagan; according to the monkish reporters, Aethelberht was a Joseph, Offa's queen a Mrs. Potiphar, Offa himself a murderer; so the rejected and inefficient seducer was canonized, and Offa forced by public opinion to raise a memorial to him.

The stranger must be warned that the triforium and clerestory of the nave are the work of the unspeakable Wyatt, who was called in to repair extensive damage wrought by the fall of a west tower. He also erected a new west front, but this was replaced by the present elaborate affair, designed by one of the Scotts. The bronze choir-screen erected by another of that clan is still perhaps admired by the untutored. Any amateur of cathedrals paying a first visit should enter by the late-Perpendicular south porch erected by Bishop Booth—whose effigy (in the nave) gives an impression of dignity and holy calm. He should then take up his stand at the central crossing and compare the strikingly contrasted styles (Norman and Decorated) of the two main transepts; look towards the east end of the choir and observe the Norman transverse arch and the enriched pier behind it; spare a curious glance for Renatus Harris's Carolean organ, the childlike Mappa Mundi in the south transept, the chained library and the mediæval reliquary known as Aethelberht's shrine; and, finally, should step into the Close and admire the lines of the Early English Lady Chapel and the proportions and rich ball-flower ornamentation of the tower (49). A delightful lane lined with queer old second-hand bookshops and antique repositories leads from the north side of the Close to the city; farther east a parallel

H

passage that bridges a lovely sunk garden links St. Ouen's Street with the Castle Grounds.

Any lover of beauty who finds himself discommoded by the *Scott*-ish west front of the cathedral can at once exchange a Victorian for a futurist atmosphere by stepping across the road—to the New Age Café, which with its bright colours, chromium and glass, amusing clock, cleverly assorted wait-resses and highly attractive manageresses, I should certainly reckon among the "sights" of Hereford to-day. Hereford also boasts a rendezvous fit for the apolaustic in the "Green Dragon" hotel. I remember lunching there once in the Three Choirs Festival week; nearly every table was graced by some dark-eyed sumptuous—or do I mean scrumptious?—prima donna: it was just when those disconcerting "eye-veils" bordered with gold and silver tissue had their first spell of vogue. Here too are proper county-town inns redolent of farming and field-sports, where you may be served by a Dickensian waiter complete with bunions and huskily-whispered advice. The "Mitre" should at least be sampled.

Hereford is a busy tourist centre, the focus of many radiat-ing roads and lines of rail; the Wye and the racecourse attract many sojourners; the spacious market place can hardly contain the market-day throngs; shops are adopting up-to-date methods of display, and engineering and other works have lately been established near the town; but what has finally banished the "always-afternoon" atmosphere from Hereford's streets is the simultaneous expansion and centralization of cider-making. Draught cider has been produced in Hereford-shire ever since the fourteenth century; it came into use during the Hundred Years' War, replacing French wines that ceased then to be imported, for cider is actually apple wine; but the making of it has till lately been essentially a farmhouse or cottage industry. Most Herefordshire farms had—many still have—cider presses (65) and subsidiary apparatus; and apple orchards are common in every part of the county. To-day, a large proportion of the cider apples is swept into the efficient jaws of Bulmer's factory; yet still you shall see in sunny angles of orchards those great heaps, or rather stacks, of ripening apples that portend the advent of the cider-making season (56).

The cider made and matured after the old fashion is potent, and possibly this persistence in the ancient ways is to be de-plored; so, at any rate, thinks one bishop; but then bishops have such extraordinary beliefs, and issue such wild pro-

62 A TYPICAL HALF-TIMBER VILLAGE: LUSTON, NEAR LEOMINSTER

63 EARDISLAND VILLAGE AND THE RIVER ARROW

64   A THATCHER AT WORK, FOWNHOPE

65   CIDER MAKING WITH AN OLD PRESS, BARTESTREE,
HEREFORDSHIRE

nouncements! In this connexion the subjoined poem should
be carefully studied—especially the final stanza.

HELL IN HEREFORDSHIRE[1]

'There is much secret cider-drinking in Herefordshire'—

(Evidence of the Bishop of Hereford before the Licensing
Commission)

The wild white rose is cankered
  Along the Vale of Lugg,
There's poison in the tankard,
  There's murder in the mug;
Through all the pleasant valleys
  Where stand the pale-faced kine
Men raise the Devil's chalice
  And drink his bitter wine.

Unspeakable carouses
  That shame the summer sky
Take place in little houses
  That look towards the Wye;
And near the Radnor border
  And the dark hills of Wales
Beelzebub is warder
  And sorcery prevails.

For, spite of church or chapel,
  Ungodly folk there be
Who pluck the cider apple
  From the cider apple-tree,
And squeeze it in their presses
  Until the juice runs out,
At various addresses
  That no one knows about.

And, maddened by the orgies
  Of that unholy brew,
They slit each other's gorges
  From one a.m. till two,
Till Ledbury is a shambles
  And in the dirt and mud
Where Leominster sits and gambles
  The dice are stained with blood!

---

[1] Reprinted by permission of the Proprietors of *Punch*.

But still, if strength suffices
Before my day is done,
I'll go and share the vices
Of Clungunford and Clun,
And watch the red sun sinking
Across the March again
And join the secret drinking
Of outlaws at Presteign.　　EVOE.

Hop-growing is almost wholly confined to the eastern part
of the shire; the district round Ledbury, for instance, and the
Teme valley below Ludford; you do not see along the border-
line those serried *quincunces* of tapered poles, criss-crossed with
cat's-cradles and diagonals of yarn (57), that constitute
modern-style hop-gardens; but as those journalists and
novelists who venture to use them as "copy" appear seldom
to have even played in hop-gardens, let alone sweated in kilns
and oast-houses, an authentic description of the preparation
of hops for market may here be acceptable.

When a garden is ready for picking, hop-bins are set along
a row: a hop-bin consists of a pair of tall trestles, joined at
waist-height by a square frame of timbers that supports a
receptacle of sacking, and at man-height by a pole placed
lengthways to support the plant-entwined hop-poles. When the
pickers are assembled, so many to each bin, labourers keep
them supplied, cutting the tough bines near the roots, pulling
up the poles and bringing them to the bins. As the garden is
gradually cleared, the bins are moved from row to row. When
the end of the working day approaches, cries of "No more
poles!"[1] and "Pick your bins!"[2] resound through the garden.
Presently the bins are emptied, bushel by bushel, into *pokes*
(bags of sacking), the tally[3] of each bin being faithfully
recorded in the presence of the farmer or a trusted foreman.

The pokes are now carted to the oast-house for drying.
The oast-house consists (primarily) of a long upper room with
a timber floor (the cooling floor) clear of all furniture except
a pressing machine at one end; into this room open two or
three hop-kilns which have floors of stout but wide-meshed
canvas stretched taut over thick narrow beams fixed edge
upwards at intervals, so spaced that the foot cannot slip
through: the kiln-floors are about four feet above the cooling-

---

[1] No more will be brought to the bins.
[2] Pick out leaves, bits of bine and dirt.
[3] Amount picked into each bin, reckoned in bushels and pecks.

floor. The commonest shape for a kiln is a square surmounted
by a cone;[1] above the cone is the heavy swinging cowl. To
watch for and at last to see the smoke issuing from the cowls
gives one a strange thrill. Under each kiln-floor is a large three-
sided furnace of brick. The ground floor of the oast-house is
usually divided into compartments, from some of which there
is ready access to the furnaces. One such compartment is the
bed-sitter of the head hop-drier, complete with beer-barrel
and plank couch mollified by two or three hop-stuffed pokes.
Of the other compartments, one is a room under the press
used for storing the *pockets*—the long cylindrical bags of
untearable, close-meshed canvas into which the hops are
pressed and in which they are dispatched. In the rest, fuel and
necessary paraphernalia are kept: the fuel includes charcoal
and brimstone.

Before the full pokes arrive from the hop-garden, the furnaces have been started. When the fires are well alight they
are continually fed with sticks of charcoal, which gives off
greater heat and far less dust than coal. The pokes are carried
up an outside ladder and across the cooling-floor, then up
shorter ladders into the kilns, where they are emptied, the
hops being spread evenly till they form a layer about knee-
high. The workers emerge; the door is shut. When all the
kilns are loaded, the furnace fires are for a time fed with fat,
yellow sticks of brimstone. The sulphur fumes kill all insects
and animalculæ lurking in the hops. To sit within sight of the
furnace fires and watch the brimstone, liquefied in the heat,
trickling through the under-bars in jets and gouts of azure
brilliance is a glamorous experience never forgotten. After a
few hours, when the fumes have quite passed away, the drying hops are turned with great wide shovels: smooth cloth
stretched on an open frame makes the blade of the shovel; the
handle soon gets blackened with a crust of hop-dust and sweat,
for the turning is terribly hot work: the furnaces are still
glowing. A few hours later, usually at 4 or 5 a.m., the kilns
are cleared, the hops being shovelled out on to the cooling-
floor and spread evenly over a space left free by the shifting
of the previous batch to the press end. Though the fires are
now dying, this kiln-clearing is still torrid work; far worse is
the necessary sweeping clean of the canvas floors; you not
only melt visibly but are parched and half-choked by the
aromatic but greasy hop-dust; however, means of washing it
down are soon forthcoming. Let any victim of chronic

[1] In Kent the oast-houses are circular in shape.

insomnia clear and sweep a kiln and then drink a quart of sound bitter; he will find that he will sleep soundly, even on the bare boards of the cooling-floor, especially if his head rests on a hop pillow.

The final operation is the pressing. *A pocket* (see above) is let down into the room below, fixed securely to an iron ring that fits the aperture under the pressing machine. The latter consists of a flat iron plate of nearly the same circumference as the pocket and fixed at the lower end of a long cogged upright bar held by a frame; the cogs correspond to cogs of a wheel that can be turned by hand. Hops are shovelled into the pocket till it is full; a catch is released by a lever and down comes the heavy plate; when it stops it is forced still farther down by the turning of the hand-wheel. Thus the hops in the pocket are squeezed into a quarter of their original volume—pressed into a sort of cake. Then more hops are shovelled in, and the press again comes into action; and so on until the pocket is full. After its mouth has been sewn up, the pocket is released to tumble into the room below, and its weight is taken. When pockets enough are ready, they are loaded on to a huge van: the "rabbits'-ears" you may have noticed at the ends of the pockets, if you have ever seen a load of hops, are not for ornament but for convenience of handling: they are stuffed with hops. At last the load moves off and begins its long journey to the borough of Southwark.

Thank God for those courageous farmers who still grow hops, and for those honest brewers who still use English hops and real barley malt!

THE DUCKING STOOL, LEOMINSTER

(Drawn by Sydney R. Jones)

66   THE RECESSES OF RADNOR FOREST: A CLOSE-UP OF THE WHIMBLE PEAK

CHAPTER VI

RADNOR FOREST AND THE RADNORS:
WITH NOTES ON THE UPPER VALLEYS OF
THE TEME AND THE LUGG

BETWEEN the Glasbury-Whitney stretch of the Wye and
Radnor Forest intervenes a labyrinth of moorlands and valleys,
a region almost wholly unknown except to its inhabitants.
Bradley calls it a "broken but delightful Arcady," adding the
sarcastic comment that every tourist following trunk roads
gives it a wide berth. Here is found a countryside isolated
from main streams of traffic, a population largely absorbed in
agriculture and stock-raising and rural sports, and lanes too
steep and narrow for motors, winding between vigorous,
intricate hedges planted on high banks that are richly dight
with unstinted profusion of wild flowers. Such hedges, such
opulent banks, are characteristic of Radnorshire.

A single main road, or rather lane, traverses the district;
climbing by steep curves from Erwood, in the Wye valley
above Boughrood, it goes undulating through Painscastle,
Newchurch and Gladestry, and finally by way of Old Radnor
reaches the modern world again at Walton, between Kington
and New Radnor. This throughway is linked with the mid
Wye valley by steep and often difficult lanes, three from near
the "Rhydspence," two from Clyro, of which one forks
almost at once, one from Llowes, and one, which soon
dwindles to a track, from Maesyronnen chapel (p. 41). From
any of these cross-lanes you get satisfying views of the Black
Mountains escarpment and Mynydd Troed, with the richly
timbered Wye valley as foreground. For the complete panorama one should ascend the Begwns, a conspicuous height
—recognizable by its fir-clump—accessible from the Llowes-
Painscastle lane or from beyond Maesyronnen chapel. The
most important Norman settlement was Painscastle, where,
under the auspices of Bernard Newmarch, lord marcher of
Brecon, Payen FitzJohn constructed a strong motte-and-
bailey. Later on Payen's Castle came into possession of the

de Braoses. William de Braose,[1] that blot upon Norman lustre, was besieged here by the warrior-poet Gwenwynwyn, Prince of Powys, who had undertaken this distant excursion in order to avenge an act of foul treachery. Henry III, when he busied himself with strengthening the Marcher fortresses, added a stone castle here to Payen's motte-and-bailey. To-day the masonry has disappeared, but the earthworks still show a bold profile and dominate the dwindled village.

Some forty years have passed since the death of the saintly but eccentric John Price, who became vicar of Llanbedr-Painscastle (so the parish is styled) in 1859. The stipend was meagre, and there was no vicarage: Price lived in three old bathing-machines (from Aberystwyth?), which served respectively as study, bedroom and kitchen.[2] The parishioners, mostly dissenters, did not find their way to church. Interpreting literally the parable of the Marriage Feast, he went out to the highways and hedges to procure guests for his spiritual banquet; and soon an offer of sixpence per head per service[3] began regularly to fill his pews with unwashed tramps and their draggle-tailed doxies. For the comfort of his flock in winter he provided oil stoves; cooking was allowed during the sermon. Price further offered five shillings to each pair of vagrants "living in sin" who would consent to let him join them in Holy Wedlock. As his sight was very weak, several business-like couples let him marry them half a dozen times. Having sunk into a very neglected state, he was taken by friends to Talgarth, where it was found necessary to cut his clothes off his skin. He did not survive the bath which followed.

Let us move on to the more cheerful Huntington, a truly Arcadian village just on the English side of the Border, and Gladestry, meeting-place of several roads, a large scattered village occupying both banks of its brook. On all sides but one it is encompassed by bold heights—ridges, sentinel hills and spur-ends—mostly mantled in woods: most conspicuous are the long Hergest ridge on the east and the "plum-pudding" Hanter Hill to north of Hergest; from the west Colva Hill

---

[1] After his time Painscastle was often known as Maud's Castle, a tribute to the personality of his wife, Maude de la Valérie. Similarly an incised monolith in Llowes churchyard is called Maud Walbee's Stone.

[2] After these were accidentally burnt down he dwelt in a brick-and-slate henhouse.

[3] Later, when he lost a tiny private income, this had to be reduced to fourpence. This new proposal was solemnly discussed in the churchyard and finally accepted by a sort of informal Tramps' Union.

descends in massive folds. In this direction an arduous lane leaving the throughway half a mile south of Gladestry repays exploration. Half-way to Colva you may look across a thick belt of trees to Cefn Hir, a cliff-terraced spur of Colva Hill, and to the moorland welter of Radnor Forest beyond it, the "engine" dome of Whimble (66) standing out clear. Colva is merely a solitary little church and some scattered farms; beyond it you pass through many-hued moorlands to Glascwm, cross the Edw at Cregrina and reach the Radnor-Builth road close to the homely and hospitable Hundred House Inn.

The northward road from Gladestry soon brings us to Old Radnor. Here is one of the most beautiful and interesting parish churches in Wales. The key is kept at a cottage beyond and below the church, which has a fine Perpendicular tower —a rarity in Wales—and stands on a hill-spur of volcanic rock, from which one looks across a green diamond of level pastures to the swelling bulk of Radnor Forest (69). The interior of the building is of unusual interest: a Perpendicular screen of delicate craftmanship extends across the breadth of the church, the aisles being continued to form chancel chapels. Four ancient stalls also remain; but a more notable example of woodwork is the Tudor organ-case, which displays several panels of "linen-fold" carving. The font has been crudely fashioned from a massive block of stone, probably the fifth monolith of the group near Knapp Farm (between Old Radnor and Kinnerton) known as "The Four Stones." A floor-slab in the chancel marking the grave of a young woman bears a gracefully pathetic inscription.

The motorists' route to the Radnors from the mid Wye valley proceeds from Whitney or Bredwardine via Eardisley and Kington. Eardisley is one long street of cottages and houses, mostly half-timbered, none very noticeable except Upper House, at the farther end, and "The Forge," on the west side. The turning left beyond the Tram Inn—wherefore *Tram*?—goes tortuously to Whitney by way of Woods Eaves, where you find cottages and small farmhouses of half-timbered work. From Eardisley a long uphill and corresponding descent bring you to the outskirts of Kington, whose High Street, narrow and often crowded, is lined with ancient houses, too many of them refronted, showing a fine irregularity of skyline; on Saturdays, market days and cattle-auction days it is colourful and lively. On the hilltop, in a wide churchyard, stands the handsome church, which has a Norman tower, once detached (notice its doorway, now within the church). The chancel is good Early English; in the Decorated south chapel is an elaborate part-alabaster tomb bearing effigies of Thomas Vaughan of Hergest,[1] who was slain on the Yorkist side at the battle of Banbury (1469), and his wife Ellen, who by a daring act of vengeance won the nickname of Gethin ("Terrible"). While still in her teens she attended a fashionable archery tournament—how early-Victorian that sounds!—and when her turn came whirled away from the target and sped her arrow through the heart of her brother's murderer.

From the road-junction near an angle of the churchyard one road is marked as leading to Hay and Gladestry. This will take you past the house where Thomas and Ellen raised a goodly brood of Vaughans. First notice on left the old grammar-school building, a pleasing specimen of John Abel's skill. Its foundress, the widow of that gallant Elizabethan sea-captain Sir John Hawkins, was a Vaughan of Hergest Court. A mile onward the road crosses the end of the Hergest ridge; here on the left is a large farmhouse, occupying a narrow rock-spur: it shows timber-framing remarkably close-set. This and a large barn are all that remain of Hergest Court: as rebuilt by Thomas Vaughan it comprised eight separate buildings— so we are told by his protegé, the poet Lewis Glan Cothi. It is partly moated by the Arrow; the Hergest ridge opposite, where it towers above the road, is crowned by earthworks known as Castle Twts. Beyond the hamlet impressively named Brilley Mountain comes a breezy expanse of hilltop common: where roads meet at its farther end choose the Hay branch. Just below the brow the "Brilley view" (15) bursts upon you: it includes all the escarpment and the great ridges of the Black Mountains, and the Brecon Beacons touching the sky to west of them. The view is seen to best effect towards the sunset of a day of light showers. Past Brilley, with a little turreted church we come to a wayside inn that proclaims itself to be in England (i.e. open on Sunday); you finally land in the Whitney-Clyro road near the "Rhydspence."

The way from Kington to New Radnor has varied elements of charm. Once clear of the town, you pass between wooded slopes descending from Hergest ridge on left and Bradnor Hill on right. Farther on, the Stanner Rocks, an abrupt and rugged volcanic mass, look across to Worsell Wood and the rounded Hanter Hill. Hence the road climbs over a spur of Old Radnor Hill, and beyond a granite quarry with crushing-mills

[1] Son of Sir Roger Vaughan of Bredwardine.

68 CLOUD OVER RADNOR FOREST, LOOKING FROM MONAUGHTY

69   THE VIEW OF RADNOR FOREST RIDGES FROM OLD RADNOR CHURCH

descends sharply to Walton, where it meets roads from Old Radnor, New Radnor, Knighton and Presteign. The heights of Radnor Forest loom large as you approach New Radnor; the smooth, bulky hill on left bears the gorgeous title of The Smatcher.

To visit the exquisite Harley Valley (11, 71)—a treat available only for walkers—follow High Street westwards past the church and turn to right along a gated path. This soon winds through a copse, emerging from which you find yourself at the mouth of the valley (not "dingle," as the postcard merchants absurdly call it); below, on left, is the little stream that carved out this vast *cwm*. Though the moorland ramparts enclosing the valley are nearly treeless, their contours and colours combine to produce a picture of undeniable charm. The track leads on through a cattle-yard, beyond which you can descry a green road mounting the opposite hillside as a diagonal shelf. You may now strike directly up Whimble, the steep dome on your right, and by descending its farther slope and climbing Bach Hill make your way to the eastern of the two Forest summits, Black Mixen; but if you wish to reach the actual highest point (the western summit, Great Rhos, 2166 ft.) you must cross the stream—I seem to remember a rough bridge of wobbly poles—and get on to the green road, from the top of which you gain the summit-plateau. Straight across the valley is the cliffy height of Great Creigiau (notice how English and Welsh are mingled in the names hereabouts); to south of it Whimble (66) bears its jutting bosom to the sky. Cross to the west side of the plateau and you look down on a tree-filled valley descending towards the Builth road; near its foot and reached by a path from that road is a waterfall queerly named Water-break-its-neck.

It is the eastern angle of Radnor Forest that offers most entertainment. The "gateway" to this district is Beggars' Bush, meeting-point of roads from New Radnor, Kington via Walton, and Knighton. From Beggars' Bush follow the Knighton road down most of the first hill, but halt at the first cross-roads, where a signpost points left to Cascob, right to Discoed and Presteign. At the cross-roads continue forward, for Cascob; after crossing a stream in about two miles, avoid right turnings, and you soon reach Cascob church, which tops a slight ascent. Notice its wild and broken background. The church is a simple structure—nave, narrow chancel and squat west tower crowned by half-timbered pyramid-capped belfry—probably of the thirteenth century; it retains a Perpendicular rood-screen. Both here and at Bleddfa (below) earth has been heaped up to form a bank enclosing the west end, probably for stability.

Some years ago, when the church was undergoing repair, the incumbent unearthed from some débris an "Abracadabra" charm against evil spirits, dated 1700; an astonishing medley of Christian sentiment, Latin doggerel and astrology, with much vain repetition. I quote bits of it *verbatim*:—"In the name of the Father, Son and of the Holy Ghost. Amen x x x and in the name of the Lord Jesus Christ who will deliver Elizabeth Loyd from all witchcraft and from all evil sprites . . . by the same power as he did cause the blind to see the lame to walke and the dum to talke. Pater pater pater noster noster noster ave ave ave Maria in secula seculorum x on x Adonay x Terragrammaton x Amen and the name of the Holy Trinnity and of Hubert . . . O Lord Jesus Christ . . . grant that this holy charm Abracadabra may cure thy survent Elizabeth Loyd from all evil sprites and all ther desesis [diseases]. Amen x x x by Jah Jah Jah."

On the north side of the Forest is Bleddfa, a scattered village amid trees; there is another Hundred House Inn, and a little thirteenth-century church, with an amusing weather-boarded belfry and fine king-post roofs.

Returning towards Presteign you have a glorious run down a charming minor valley till at the first crossways, meeting-place of roads from Knighton and Presteign, you enter the Lugg valley. About a mile beyond the road-junction, half-way to Whitton, look out for a church on left, with a mansion near it. This is Pilleth church: mounds in the river-meadows below the road mark resting-places of English dead. There in 1401 a Welsh force under Glyndwr's chief captain, Rhys Gethin, defeated with heavy slaughter troops led by Edmund Mortimer, uncle of the future Edward IV. Mortimer was captured, imprisoned by Glyndwr, and married to one of Glyndwr's valuable daughters. Shakespeare is glancing at Pilleth when he writes of:

"A post from Wales laden with heavy news."

Beyond Pilleth you soon reach another crossways at three-sheltered Whitton. Hence you may continue down the Lugg valley to Presteign; or turn right for New Radnor (the longer route, by Walton, is the easier for cyclists); or turn left for Knighton. Let us follow this last route. After a stiff climb over the flank of Cwm Whitton Hill (p. 71) comes a long smooth descent to Knighton, which town, so soon as you can see it clearly, reveals itself as a long huddle of blue-slated and red-tiled roofs in a trough-like valley; it would make a good drop-scene in the Cubist style (79). Farther on, the timber belfry-stage of the church's Norman tower swims into your ken. Prosperous villas fringe the outskirts of the town, which you enter still descending, then, after passing between rival inns, you must climb again towards one of those dreadful municipal clock-towers, all made to one repulsive pattern, of which so many Welsh towns possess a specimen—Hay, Rhayader, Machynlleth, Ruthin, to name a few. The essential business of Knighton centres on its acres of market-pens, for here important sales of stock are held.

From the clock tower A483 climbs over Bailey Hill to the Lugg valley and Bleddfa; the forward road ascends the Teme valley, and an interesting excursion can be made in this direction. After the last houses of Knighton have been left behind the valley widens to a miniature plain, though the river itself winds along close under the road. The valley narrows again, and rounding a corner beyond a railway bridge you are surprised to see a range of tall narrow towers pierced with arrow slits and crowned with stagey battlements. A closer look shows these Victorian erections to be the piers of a railway viaduct. Do not pass under the viaduct, but turn sharp right and cross to the left bank of the river. On this side of the Teme we are in Shropshire, which throws out an extensive bulge towards Wales, outlined roughly by the Upper Teme and the summit-ridge of Clun Forest. We approach Llanvair Waterdine, merely a rebuilt church, an inn and scattered farms; a very heraldic red lion treated in the modern manner beckons you confidently from the inn-sign. Across the river a ridge descends boldly to a cluster of cottages; on the hither side, above the road, cattle graze peacefully in broad meadows backed by woodlands. Looking up the valley you see a welter of hill-spurs, with the long line of Kerry Hill in the purple distance. Farther up the valley lies Beguildy, on the Radnorshire side; to reach it we must go back and recross the Teme. Beguildy church retains a beautiful Perpendicular rood-screen with traceried panels and elaborate carving, other fine woodwork, too—a handsome Jacobean pulpit, an altar-table of the same period and a more ancient bench-end.

From Beguildy one may continue forward, through scenery of increasing wildness, to the top of the valley, cross the end of Kerry Hill, and descend by steep zigzags to Newtown

(p. 85) in the Severn Valley. Kerry Hill is a valuable breeding-ground of rivers. The Teme, the Clun, the Ithon and the Mule all rise on Kerry Hill; the Lugg on Beacon Hill, the massive moorland south of Beguildy. The Clun joins the Teme at Leintwardine (p. 72), and the Teme flows into the Severn just below Worcester; the Lugg enters the Wye at Mordiford below Hereford. The extensive moorland drained by the upper valleys of these streams is what geographers call a dissected plateau and has few heights rising above the 1700 ft. contour, but is far from monotonous.

An unfrequented route from Knucklas southwards takes one through interesting country quite unknown even to the enterprising tourist. For this, you must first pass under the viaduct. Forward again till you reach the small "spiky"-looking church of Heyop, a little short of which a rough lane goes off to left towards a belt of wood; this will take you over Bailey Hill. Among confusing tracks at the road-top choose the one descending forward: you should soon find a deepening valley on your left and should be able to descry, beyond copses and scattered trees and, in the foreground, a belt of giant foxgloves, the sweeping curves of Radnor Forest. Now comes a rapid descent to the upper Lugg valley; from half-way down you catch sight of a largish village—Llangunllo—which from this point looks truly attractive. The charm of Llangunllo by no means vanishes on a closer view, but rather is enhanced by the high average of comeliness among its children and young women. Excellent roads follow the course of the Lugg all the way hence to Presteign. At the ensuing crossways our road meets that from Bleddfa, and we continue past Pilleth and through Whitton (p. 68).

Presteign (77) is one of the most charming of the smaller Welsh towns, and having ready access to Radnor Forest, the "black-and-white" country, the Deerfold Forest region, the middle valley of the Wye, and the Shropshire Highlands, is a useful strategic centre for the lover of varied scenery. Here is a comfortable inn, the Radnorshire Arms (74), a genuine half-timbered antique, once owned by a relative of that Bradshaw who signed the "martyred" Charles's death-warrant; and there is abundance of humbler accommodation. The average of physical beauty is here again high. It chanced that I passed through the town on the day of George V's Jubilee, celebrated here by a children's fancy-dress carnival; the majority of the youngsters were strikingly attractive. Another surprising thing I have remarked about Presteign, and its

70 MAESMELAN FARM AT FOOT OF RADNOR FOREST

71 IN THE HARLEY VALLEY, RADNOR FOREST

72 A WATERSPLASH ON THE HINDWELL BROOK, KNILL

73 THE CHURCH, BRAMPTON BRYAN, IN THE TEME VALLEY

neighbours Kington and Knighton as well, is the enthusiasm for cricket shown by the younger inhabitants—a genuine enthusiasm, for in this "dizzy" countryside you cannot evolve a decent pitch without labour and sacrifice.

The turning that leads to the church is a broad dignified street of seemly Georgian houses, now mostly used for professional offices. The church is a large imposing structure, of Norman origin but remodelled in the Decorated period. The Warden, a public open space, contains the site of the castle.

Several of the approach-ways to Presteign are of unusual beauty and interest. From Kington you may go either directly through Titley or by a detour through Walton. The former route begins with a long climb, then descends past the lovely demesne of Eywood, rich in ornamental waters and secular trees, beyond which, close to the road, stands The Rodd, a wonderful Jacobean manor-house, with period interior retaining panelled walls, carved plaster ceilings and elaborate chimney-pieces, one of them extraordinarily elaborate. The road from Walton, after crossing two streams which converge to form the Hindwell Brook, runs along the north side of the latter's straight narrow valley, below a succession of thickly wooded heights; across the valley is Little Brampton Scar, a line of tree-clad cliffs. Watch for a lane descending to right, bordered by trees perfectly matched in size and shape and planted with precise regularity. This leads to Knill; near its foot, but beyond the farther side of the church, you shall find Knill Court, half-timbered and richly gabled, Elizabethan but with a fourteenth-century core. For a spectacular route from Knighton, follow the Kington road to the Rhos-y-meirch road-fork, at the top of the first long hill; there choose the left branch, which crosses Cwm Whitton Hill at the height of 1208 ft., then descends shelf-wise above a deep gorge across which rise Stonewall Hill and, beyond it, Harley's Mountain. Much of Cwm Whitton Hill is Government property and is used for agricultural and botanical experiments directed towards the improvement of upland pastures.

The road (A4113) from Knighton to Brampton Bryan and Leintwardine along the right bank of the Teme forms a link with a district of Shropshire described in the next chapter. Two miles from Knighton a lane to left leads across the river to Stow, a child's-picture-book village nestling in a cwm of Stow Hill. Not far away is Bucknell, like Stow just in Shropshire; there is a marvellous view from Bucknell Hill's 1000 ft., overlooking the idyllic Chapel lawn valley which strikes off the Knighton-Clun road. The main road skirts Stanage Park, a demesne of swelling contours and ancient timber, and presently enters Brampton Bryan village (73). From the churchyard you may contrive to get a peep of the castle, otherwise rigorously shielded from the vulgar gaze; it consists of a modern mansion and, adjoining it, the ruins of the ancient castle of the Harleys, celebrated for its stubborn defence under the heroic Lady Brilliana Harley against a Royalist besieging force. The castle park lies to south of the road; from a footpath that leads across it and traverses a wooded slope beyond it, finally descending to Boresford at the foot of Harley's Mountain (p. 71), distant views of the castle may be obtained.

Opposite the village, on the farther bank of the Teme, rises Coxall Knoll, one of several Border heights identified with the scene (as described by Tacitus) of Caratacus's last stand against the Roman legions. Many such identifications are clearly wrong: Tacitus's "stream hard to ford" is lacking. Coxall Knoll seems to fulfil the requirements.

The massive, rather gaunt tower of Leintwardine church is clearly visible long before you reach the little town. This you enter by a delightful bridge over the Teme (76), which has just received the waters of the Clun and here broadens to a pool frequented by the local ducks. The first building on left is the principal hotel, a pleasant place of low-ceilinged rooms. Once its trim parlourmaid, pardonably doubtful of my solvency—I must have resembled the "tramp cyclist"—warned me that a plain tea was one-and-six. The town consists of little more than two parallel streets mounting a fairly steep slope; between them is the church, which contains carved stalls from Wigmore Abbey. The tower has on the west face a conspicuous stair-turret. Leintwardine was a Roman station (Bravonium); remains still survive in some cottage gardens.

From Leintwardine one may strike north to Craven Arms, south to Wigmore and Leominster, or east to Ludlow either by a right turn beyond the top of the town over Fiddler's Elbow to Bromfield or by the more attractive if even more arduous route via Burrington and Bringewood Chase (67, 81). Near Downton on the Rock is the Hay Mill where the Teme rushes through a wildly picturesque wooded gorge on its way to the grounds of Downton Castle; the gorge may be visited on Tuesdays. Just short of Burrington the Teme is crossed by a tall stone bridge; approaching it, you may contemplate at leisure the two lines of well-wooded hills—Bringe-

74   THE RADNORSHIRE ARMS, PRESTEIGN

75   THE JACOBEAN GATEHOUSE, STOKESAY CASTLE

76 THE RIVER TEME WITH THE BRIDGE AND INN, LEINTWARDINE

77 IN BROAD STREET, PRESTEIGN, THE VILLAGE CAPITAL
OF RADNORSHIRE

wood Chase (left) and High Vinnalls (right) with its clump-crowned satellites—converging merrythought-fashion towards Ludlow. The charming picture is completed by a glimpse of the bridge and Burrington church tower (67). Meeting the Wigmore-Ludlow road near Aston, you cross the shoulder of Bringewood Chase, passing near the top of Mary Knowl with its glorious sweeping view; at its foot in the forest by "Sunny Gutter" two Sidney children suffered that terrifying experience which inspired Milton's *Comus*. Prospects are rather limited by trees, but as you descend above the limestone scarps of the Whitcliff, you enjoy a glorious birds'-eye view of Ludlow and its historic castle (6, 78). Presently you are crossing Ludford Bridge and have before you Ludlow's ancient Broad Gate.

THE GATEWAY, WIGMORE ABBEY
(Drawn by H. T. Timmins)

K

CHAPTER VII

THE SHROPSHIRE HIGHLANDS AND
ADJACENT PARTS OF WALES. SOUTHERN
SECTION: LUDLOW, CRAVEN ARMS, CLUN
AND MONTGOMERY DISTRICTS

THAT part of Shropshire which lies between the Severn and
the Welsh Border contrasts in a striking manner with the rest
of the shire. The difference in physical configuration has its
underlying cause in geological structure, the district south
and west of the great river being, like most of Wales, largely
formed of rocks not later than of Carboniferous age, with
several igneous patches; the north and east of the county, of
later rocks. In the extreme south-west is the great Silurian
bulge that includes Clun Forest; north and east of this come
numerous ridges running north-eastward: farthest north, Long
Mountain (5), continued in Montgomeryshire by the Breiddens (97); then in succession Corndon and Stapeley Hills, the
Stiperstones ridge (87, 106), the Longmynd (92, 93), the Caer
Caradoc "range" (92, 94) and, longest of all, Wenlock Edge,
which is flanked by two lovely valleys, Ape Dale (80, 86) and
Corve Dale. South-east of the Edge, again, but with north-to-
south axis, come the twin peaks of the Clee Hills (78). Finally
there are (in Herefordshire) the lines of hills converging on
Ludlow like the arms of a merrythought and, linking the
ends of the two arms, the tangled uplands of Wigmore Rolls
and Deerfold Forest.

These Shropshire Highlands, never very high, but almost
worthy of the name of mountains through their impressive
outlines and "dizzy" slopes, offer a diversity of scenery that
ranges from the almost startling—the first sight of the Breiddens (97), for instance, or the view from Wenlock Edge down
into Ape Dale (80, 86)—to the truly exquisite, as examples of
which may be given the outline of Corndon Hill, the pastures
and woods of Corve Dale and the wonderful Cardingmill
Valley. Roads in the district are generally excellent and, where
hilly, skilfully gradiented; and the wilder country of hilltop
and deep wood is criss-crossed with a tangle of lanes, cart-

78 LUDLOW: THE CASTLE WALLS AND ST. LAWRENCE'S TOWER BACKED BY THE TWIN CLEE HILLS

79 THE TOWN OF KNIGHTON IN THE TEME VALLEY, RADNORSHIRE

tracks and footpaths that offer perpetual possibilities to the
indefatigable pedestrian, or even cyclist roughrider. Among
good strategic centres for the study and enjoyment of this part
of the Borderland are Woofferton, Ludlow, Craven Arms, the
Strettons and the Clun villages; for the western "bulge," Clun
and Bishop's Castle; for Corndon Hill and Long Mountain,
Montgomery. These places provide good hotel and "guest-
house" accommodation; or if you wish to be quite sequestered,
you may not infrequently find a farmhouse that will receive
a boarder.

   In the preceding chapter mention has been made of
Richard's Castle. This lies at the edge of a most perplexing bit
of country, and as a preliminary to its exploration a general
grasp of its lay-out is useful. Its main features are the two
arms of the "merrythought," Bringewood Chase (67, 81),
which runs westwards from Ludlow towards Leintwardine,
and the ridge extending from High Vinnalls south-west towards Wigmore. But this latter ridge throws off, half-way
along its course, a roughly parallel ridge which towards its
westward termination again divides into a short northern arm
(Croft Ambrey) descending to Yatton and a longer southern
arm that ends opposite Mortimer's Cross. In the deep valley
between the parallel ridges is Leinthall Earls; in the broad
triangular lowland between the Bringewood and Vinnals
ridges are Leinthall Starkes, Burrington (67) (p. 74), and,
on the farther side north of Wigmore, Adforton (81) and
Wigmore Abbey. Presteign offers another fine triangular
vale (2), but by Wigmore is an actual stretch of fen grazing, a
miniature Otmoor, which it is purgatorial or indeed actually
impracticable to cross. The ridges are mantled in almost continuous woods; Croft Ambrey is crowned by a mighty earthwork and has several noble clumps of trees. The lower northern
end of Bringewood Chase merges into the splendid grounds
of Downton Castle (eighteenth-century Gothic), which were
laid out anew by the first Knight owner. The forested gorge
of the Teme at Hay Mill, Downton (p. 72), is worth more
than a cursory glance.

   Routes traversing a rich diversity of scenery lead from the
Teme valley below Ludlow to the Leinthalls. Part of this
district bears the sonorous name of The Goggin, and includes
the breakneck Killhorse Lane. An intricate hilly way leads
from Woofferton to Leinthall Earls, in its later stages passing
between a thick belt of trees and a vast meadow backed by a
wood and often populous with cattle. Then comes a fork: the

right branch, with gates and lodge at its entry, is a back way
to Tudor Gatley Park; the left track, a rough, very steep
descent known as The Wylde, will bring you to Leinthall
Earls, approaching which look upwards to left for the wall-
like Croft Ambrey whaleback and to right for the imposing,
finely-situated mansion of Gatley Park. From the next hamlet,
Yatton, you get a good end-on view of Croft Ambrey.
Beyond Yatton you come into the main road between Wigmore and Aymestrey. Footpaths lead over Bircher Common
by the side of Croft Ambrey; they afford incomparable views.

Leinthall Starkes, larger and less primitive-looking than
the other Leinthall, lies on the Ludlow-Wigmore highway.
Wigmore has seen better days—or, at any rate, more exciting
and colourful days. It is strange to reflect that for centuries
the streets of this now peaceful, almost sleepy village were
constantly trodden not only by men-at-arms and liveried retainers of the great House of Mortimer, but by glittering
cavalcades of knightly warriors, by palfreys bearing delicately
nurtured women, by furtive political plotters and go-betweens,
by the sober retinues of grave counsellors and ecclesiastics.

The church and the castle ruins are approached by lanes.
Grassy mounds and ridges reveal the once great extent of the
fortress-dwelling: the masonry remains, overgrown with ivy
and brambles and bosomed in trees, are even for the expert
antiquarian hard to decipher; the amateur gets a confused
impression from which only a resounding gateway-arch and a
shattered keep crowning a high mound stands out clearly.

From the villages strikes off an old road known as Barnett
Lane, which passes between Wigmore Rolls (north) and the
extensive Barnett Wood. From a meeting-place of tracks
beyond the wood a double turn left, along a rivulet, brings
you to Chapel Farm, one of Sir John Oldcastle's refuges: the
house retains a fifteenth-century roof and a "Lollard's table"
—actually a prime specimen of *Jacobean* carving. Barnett Lane
meets the Lingen-Leintwardine road near Birtley, south of
Brampton Bryan. Southward the latter road curves round the
base of Coles Hill, passes Kinsham—Florence Nightingale
spent some of her childhood at Kinsham Court—and after
crossing the Lugg climbs to meet the Shobdon-Presteign
road at Broad Heath, at the foot of Wapley Hill (2), with its
large triangular camp with quadruple earthwork defences.
From above Broad Heath delightful views are revealed
towards Presteign and towards Lingen.

The Wigmore-Lingen road, metalled but mostly very

hilly, after a long rise bends south to skirt Barnett Wood. If you leave the road at this point and make your way south-wards up through a new Government plantation to a bare hump known as Oakley Top, you will be rewarded with a marvellous general view of Deerfold Forest and surrounding hills, with Radnor Forest on the horizon. On its south side the hump drops abruptly if not quite precipitously to the Aymestrey-Lingen track beyond Lower Lye (p. 78), and on its outskirts are very lonely farms—Woolhampton, Mistletoe Oak, and one mysteriously named The Old Shop. "Deerfold Forest" is not a precise topographical term, but may here be taken to include the tangle of hills, woods and streams—in-cluding the Lugg—lying within the area bounded by the points Wigmore, Mortimer's Cross, Shobdon Hill and Lingen. The Wigmore-Lingen way, beyond the point where we left it, crosses a stream, climbs a long bank past a row of rather grim-looking cottages suggestively named Hunger Street, to road-top crossways known as "Cross-of-the-Tree," where there *is* a tree—a sturdy oak. At Lingen turn right and, beyond the church, left; you are then on another rough lane that rises to 936 ft.; it brings you to Presteign, with a splendid view of Radnor Forest from beyond the road-top; the descent cul-minates in a "surprise" view of Stapleton Castle—walls and clustered chimneys of a Tudor house occupying the site of a Border fortress on the crest of a pine-fringed cliff.

Deerfold Forest, without being spectacular, is one of the most delightful and inexhaustible rambling-grounds on the whole Border. It is traversed by a flat-bottomed gorge watered by the Lugg and winding between steep pine-wooded bluffs. To get the general "hang" of the district follow a passable road—fit for tough cyclists or in part small cars—that starts from the Shobdon road a little west of Mortimer's Cross. This undulates past a large-sized farmhouse, Covenhope; de-scends gently to the Lugg gorge, where it coalesces with a faint track that has come from Aymestrey along the *south* bank of the river[1]; then crosses the Lugg by a stone bridge and mounts steeply up a bumpy hill to the group of roomy farm-houses and cottages known as Upper Lye, beyond which you take a mere waterworn hill-track, hard going till you reach "The Camp," a briar-grown tump, which is the highest point (940 ft.) of Deerfold Forest; hence you enjoy spacious views southwards over the lowland between Pembridge and Leominster and westwards of the welter of hills round Pres-

[1] This track is apt to be terribly muddy, and is not recommended.

teign. Even more richly beautiful is the prospect from the gorse-dotted hillside reached by following a green track running left. The main track after passing a ruined chapel brings you into the Wigmore-Lingen road at Cross-of-the-Tree (*ante*).

Another pleasant route is the old Aymestrey-Lingen road, starting near the *north* end of the Lugg bridge at Aymestrey (89), it follows the left bank of the river for a mile, then ascends beside a tributary to Lower Lye; skirts the west flank of the "hump" previously mentioned (p. 77), which towers above it like a wall, and finally joins the Covenhope route just short of Cross-of-the-Tree. The Aymestrey Bridge is a charming spot. At its south end is a roomy black-and-white inn; from a gate opposite, or from the bridge, you look on the beautiful gardens and ornamental river-fed pools of Yatton Court. My impression of idle minutes spent here includes water-lilies floating on a pool, bright-hued flower-beds, a stately mansion backed by a low ridge, tall trees fringing an emerald lawn, little pink pigs clamouring round the gate, and two comely young women in not unbecoming shorts earnestly studying a map spread on the bridge wall.

Between Wigmore and Brampton Bryan lies Adforton (81), another half-timbered village, near which is a turning east, leading to Wigmore Grange and Burrington (67) (p. 72). Wigmore Grange is the relic of a priory originally founded nearer Wigmore. Observant monks noted that the land near Adforton was more fertile than what they had been granted; and the founder, Hugh, son of the first Ralph Mortimer, was persuaded to remove the priory to this favoured site. A feeble creature, he had feebly opposed Henry II, and ended his days as a canon of his new foundation. His son Roger, a man of sterner stuff, threatened to revoke the grant, but knuckled under to ecclesiastical pressure when his wife had an illness after childbirth. The remains of the priory, now mingled with farm buildings, comprise the gatehouse—a stone archway surmounted by a timber-framed overhanging storey (p. 73)—and a guest-house with open timber roof and traceried window.

The route from Wigmore over Bringewood Chase makes the best initial approach to Ludlow, since it includes the Whitcliff, whence the town is seen as in a plan, and has its proper background—the Clee Hills (6, 78). The enthralling if not quite historical history of Fulk Fitzwarine's connexion with Ludlow Castle is the theme of a famous French *roman*, and need not be retold here; and there are adequate local guide-

80   LOOKING ACROSS TO THE WREKIN FROM THE NORTH END OF WENLOCK EDGE

81 THE BRINGEWOOD CHASE HEIGHTS FROM ADFORTON

books to both castle and parish church. The visitor will be well advised to see the view from the summit of Roger de Lacy's keep. Border lawlessness and the Lords Marchers' autonomous power first felt the bonds of restraint when Edward IV established here the Court of the Marches.[1] Arthur, Henry VII's eldest son, whose early betrothal to Catherine of Aragon led indirectly to England's breach with Rome, was sent here for safety while the new dynasty was still in danger from pretenders. "Prince Arthur's Room" is shown in the north-west tower[2]; close by is the great hall in which Milton's masque of *Comus* was first acted; it was recently revived with a company (it is said) of some six thousand.

The cathedral-like Church of St. Lawrence (78, 85), whose noble Perpendicular tower is visible miles away, should be approached by way of The Scallens and the octagonal south porch. Even Nonconformist hikers must be stirred to admiration by the poppy-heads and grotesque misericords of the collegiate stalls; the superb rood-screen and loft; and the wealth of ancient glass, whereby St. Lawrence's fiery martyrdom is depicted in the great east window, and the Apostles' Creed and the story of Edward the Confessor's ring in windows of St. John's Chapel. The sightseer's list should include the "Reader's House" (by the church) and Lane's Hospital; the fourteenth-century Grammar School; the Elizabethan Castle Lodge; the odd-looking Butter Cross (with clock turret) (85); and the famous "Feathers" and "Angel" inns, pre-eminent examples of half-timbered construction. But what vandal has spoilt the elaborate frontage of the "Feathers" by inserting a plinth of dark-red sanitary tiles?

Of the ancient town gates, Broad Gate remains, spanning Broad Street; this thoroughfare slopes down to Ludford Bridge and is lined with solid Georgian buildings, once the town houses of local gentry (85). At Ludford, just across the Teme, notice the gables and chimneys of St. Giles's Hospital (rebuilt 1672), Ludford House, which embodies work of the thirteenth century, the former Bell Inn (half-timbered) and, in the church, the Foxe tomb.

The Clee Hills (78), Ludlow's eastern guardians, are extinct volcanoes, and are crowned with deep caps of basalt that provide the valuable road-metal known as *dhu* stone. Brown Clee, the northern peak, has two summits, Abdon Burf (1792 ft.) and Clee Burf; Titterstone Clee is itself crowned by a large pre-

[1] Its winter sessions were held at Bewdley.
[2] His "tomb" in the church is probably not authentic.

historic camp ringed with a *vallum* of loose stones and containing traces of pit-dwellings and hut-circles; a similar camp on Abdon Burf has been destroyed by quarrying. The Brown Clee slopes are approached (geographically) by a long ridgeway mysteriously called The Thrift; however, anyone but the stoutest hearted and shod ridge-tramper will follow the delightful hilly lanes past Abdon, till the slopes of the Brown Clee are reached at the exact 1000 ft. line. There is a glorious westward view, over the broad pastures of Corve Dale, with the wavy Stretton summits over the holts of Wenlock Edge, and the tangled Welsh hills closing in the horizon. Rounding the northern edge of the bulky hill, there is a dramatic contrast: the bare moorland slopes are replaced by groves and plantations, far-flung masses of woodland, laid out by a former Lord Boyne of Burwarton for his bride. The view has changed with equal suddenness—the eye ranges over an immense stretch of the rolling midland plain, on occasion of an intense blue, till the smoke-haze of the Black-Country towns mists the sky-line. On the slopes and spurs of these hills are several villages, sequestered and peaceful except for a patchy invasion by imported quarrymen. They bear names typical of rural England, such as Clee St. Margaret (perhaps the prettiest of the villages), with its water lane, fascinating if not impassable, Aston Botterel, Hope Baggot, Hopton Wafers, Stottesdon, Lubberland, Ditton Priors and Stoke St. Milborough (named after the Saxon princess Milburga, foundress of Wenlock Priory). But greater attractions of this secluded district are the perfect simple little Norman Heath Chapel in a field (90) and the fine early camp at Nordy Bank. Cold Weston is the loneliest of little churches and Hopton Cangeford has a Georgian church of unknown dedication with a squire's pew complete with fireplace and red curtains.

Bromfield, on the way from Ludlow to Craven Arms has a once monastic church showing work of the four great periods and also a seventeenth-century arched ceiling painted with coats-of-arms. Part of a monastic gateway still remains. Beside the churchyard the Onny flows into the Teme; across the latter is the spacious park of Oakley Hall, laid out in naturalistic style by one of the Knights. The Ludlow racecourse is in this parish; across its barrow-dotted level expanse lies the rough shaggy upland known as Hayton's Bent, bounding Corve Dale to the north. Here is Stanton Lacey church, with more than a trace of Saxon work, and Culmington, with a curiously truncated broach spire. Above Bromfield the Onny

82 LOOKING NORTHWARD TO THE HILLS FROM WIGMORE
CASTLE KEEP

84 HOPESAY CHURCH, HIDDEN IN ITS VALLEY NEAR CRAVEN ARMS

84 BROAD STREET, LUDLOW, WITH ITS GEORGIAN HOUSES 1 TO 7 AWARDING CHILDE
FLUING SCANDARDS CHURCH

valleys runs straitened between wooded bluffs, but opens out before we reach Stokesay Castle (75, 88).

This is in the literal sense a picturesque building: it is also the earliest intact example of a fortified manor-house. In 1291 a mere merchant, one Laurence of Ludlow (not "de Ludlow": the *de* of the charter is Latin, not French), having acquired the manor and set up as a gentleman, obtained a "licence to crenellate," and so added embattled walls and north and south towers to the already existing hall and solar. The lovely half-timbered gatehouse is Elizabethan (75); the timber-framed upper storey of the north tower dates from the Great Rebellion, when also the curtain walls were demolished. Before that, the castle had been repaired by that Lord Craven who so fondly loved Elizabeth of Bohemia: he had hoped she might dwell here, but after her death he built a fine new mansion on the Berkshire downs, Hampstead Marshall, where only its gatepiers dot the fields, but it lives again for us in Kip's view. The older of the Craven Arms inns was named after the enamoured nobleman, and later the hamlet and the railway station after the inn.

Craven Arms is a meeting-place of railway lines from Builth and Knighton, Ludlow, Shrewsbury (via Church Stretton), Ironbridge, Shifnal and, now disused, Bishop's Castle, and of main roads from all these towns and from Much Wenlock, Bridgnorth and Clun. The queer old signpost opposite the older inn (now a P.R.H.A. house) gives further information, but its mileages are impressionistic. Owing to its strategic central position the village has developed into an important stock mart; it seems at the first horrified glance to consist chiefly of vast zinc-roofed sheds; but one can immediately exchange these for sylvan and pastoral beauties by turning up the Much Wenlock road. This pleasant highway takes you up one side of Corve Dale at a height sufficient for wide views. Features of the route are the noble parks of Culmington Manor, Corfton and Diddlebury Halls, Millichope Park and Lutwyche Hall; two romantic old inns at Munslow; and Shipton Court,[1] (p. 86), a flawless gem of Elizabethan architecture, with a lovely terraced garden. A fitting climax is enjoyed if you turn left at the next hamlet, Brockton, and on reaching the parallel road, beyond Easthope, mount the left bank and look down over the actual *edge* of Wenlock Edge into Ape Dale. Two remarkable ancient houses near the route sketched above are Elsich (1545), approached by a lane lead-

[1] Long held by Myttons—not the branch that produced "Jack."

L

ing south from "Pedlar's Rest," near the Ludlow turn, and
Upper Millichope (on the Rushbury road), one of the oldest
houses in Britain. In Norman times this was the dwelling of
the verderer of Long Forest, which covered the Edge and its
skirting valleys. It retains early windows (with a slot to bar
the shutters), doorway, and a stone stairway in the thickness
of a wall: two of the arches were later embellished with the
ball-flower. Wilderhope, the fine four-square mansion of the
Smallmans, with its circular wooden stair and modelled
plaster ceilings has, after a period of neglect, been turned
into a Youth Hostel.

The broken country lying between the nearer ends of the

THE TOWER DWELLING OF UPPER MILLICHOPE
(Drawn by H. T. Timmins)

chief Shropshire
ridges and the eastern
side of Clun Forest
affords scope for an
interesting, not too
long, circular tour
from Craven Arms.
Start by the Church
Stretton road but turn
west at Cheney Long-
ville. Beyond Hor-
derley comes a quite
pleasant stretch where
you have the heathery,
rock-strewn terminal
slope of the Long-
mynd on right and
the spreading woods
of Plowden Hall on

left. Here starts a ridgeway—The Portway, not too rough
for small cars — which runs right along the backbone of
the Longmynd to Leebotwood, ten miles away at the
northern end. Tiny sequestered Myndtown lies on a knoll
below; but the authentic Saxon settlement is at Minton (p. 89),
on the opposite flank of the Longmynd. The *mynd* (or *min*)
element in these three names is the Welsh *mynydd*, mountain
ridge or group.

You may proceed to Bishop's Castle direct or by a detour
through Lea, where a mediæval keep stands closely girt with
buildings of an Elizabethan farmhouse. Lea Castle was an outwork of the actual bishop's castle, which stood at the top of
the town so named on a site that is now a fine bowling green

86   APE DALE, FROM WENLOCK EDGE, LOOKING TO THE
STRETTON HILLS

87 SQUILVER HILL AND HEATH MYND SOUTH OF THE STIPERSTONES, SHROPSHIRE

—still retaining portions of curtain-wall—attached to the principal inn. Near by is a cupolaed Georgian town-hall, from which a long street of irregular skylines and frontages descends to the church. This retains its massive ancient tower; as for the rest of it, the date of rebuilding—1860—explains but does not excuse the chancel ceiling.

Lydbury North, Clunbury, Hopton Castle and Clungunford may comfortably be included in a return route. Within the first-named parish are three ancient demesnes, Oakeley, Walcot and Plowden (p. 82). The Walcot estate was purchased by the great Lord Clive and passed to the Earls of Powis[1] through the marriage of his grandson to a Herbert lady: the mansion has been demolished since the War. Lydbury North church has one of the fortress-like towers often seen hereabouts (91).

At cross-roads beyond Lydbury North turn southwards along the little Kemp valley for Clunbury, a village of somnolent rusticity lying between the river Clun and Clunbury Hill (83). Rounding Clunbury Hill you reach Hopton Castle village; the castle stands close to the road on low ground; it resembles a Northumbrian peel-tower, and is actually the Norman keep of a once extensive fortress. Held successively by Cliffords, Mortimers, Corbets and Wallops, it was the scene of a tragedy during the Great Rebellion, when its Royalist defenders were "executed" to a man for defending the indefensible. The hill behind the castle displaying a curiously nicked summit, like Devilsbit Mountain in Ireland, is Hopton Titterhill. The lane crossing the Clun valley to Clungunford passes near Beckjay Mill, which figures in more than one painting by David Cox. Abcott House near Clungunford, and Heath House and Broadward House, between the village and Leintwardine, are truly picturesque mansions with interesting interiors: Heath House has a marvellous oak staircase (p. 106).

In writing of this district I feel bound to quote again the oft quoted:

> Clunton and Clunbury, Clungunford and Clun
> Are the ˉ ˘ -est places under the sun.

The superlative may be completed according to fancy; two of the politer variants are "quietest" and "sleepiest."

For a longer and more adventurous circular trip from Craven Arms I can from personal experience recommend

---

[1] Who are thus by male descent Clives, not Herberts.

the route via Clun through the wilds of Clun Forest to its
summit-ridge, then down to Kerry or Newtown and back by
Montgomery and Church Stoke. Leaving Craven Arms the
Clun road reaches the Clun valley at Aston-on-Clun,[1] and
mounts gently beside the river past the smiling gardens of
Purslow Hall and, beyond Clunton, between richly wooded
slopes that receded as you approach Clun. The rather forlorn
townlet of to-day is graced by the gables, chimneys and dormer
windows of Holy Trinity Hospital, founded in 1614 by one
of the Howards. The fortress-like tower of the church, like
others of the Border, has a pyramidal cap interrupted hori-
zontally by a line of louvred openings; inside, a pyx-canopy
—rare feature—hangs above the east window. Near the
Buffalo Inn, where Scott once stayed in order to get local
colour for *The Betrothed*, the Clun is crossed by an ancient
bridge of irregular arches. On the north bank stand the
castle ruins—a lofty Norman keep lacking one wall, but
rising stark and grim from its knoll, with fragments of two
other towers and a curtain wall.

Clun Forest, an undulating moorland sprinkled with upland
pastures and intakes, copses and belts of trees, is traversed
from east to west by the river Clun, the course of which is
followed closely by a passable road. The Forest and adjacent
Kerry Hill are noted for prehistoric relics—camps and stone
circles—and for the famous Clun Forest and Kerry Hill breeds
of mountain sheep. Nearing Newcastle, the half-way village,
you will descry Offa's Dyke descending either hillside; well
beyond the village a breakneck lane starts up on left for
Bettws-y-Crwyn,[2] where the church, one of the highest—
speaking physically—in England, retains a Perpendicular
screen (p. 116), a timber chancel roof of handsome pattern
and a marvellous silver chalice of 1655 (queer date for such an
object) with repoussé ornament. Tracks lead hence southwards to Beguildy in the Teme valley. The main road beside
the Clun mounts, more steeply now, past Hall-of-the-Forest,
a Tudor farmhouse built by a FitzAlan's widow, to the lonely,
windswept Anchor Inn, concerning which Miss Magdalene
Weale tells such an amusing yarn, in her splendid *Through the
Shropshire Highlands on Horseback*. In more senses than one
the "Anchor" is the "Last House in England"; but to reach

[1] Whence a lane leads north to Hopesay, a little village in a wooded hollow
almost encircled by hills (84). The approach view makes a pretty picture.
[2] In Shropshire in spite of its Welsh name, which means "Prayer-house of the
Skins" (or fleeces): the church had as a rule congregations of rough shepherds.

the actual crest of the moor we still have to cross a hollow of heather and bog-pools and climb to the summit-ridge, here called Kerry Pole.

From Kerry Hill the road descends rapidly along the flank of a wooded *cwm*, then winds along more gently into Kerry. The valley glimpsed ahead is that of the Severn. On the west side, away from the road, stands the parish church, which strongly resembles that of Clun. The churchyard was the scene of the famous encounter between a Bishop of St. Asaph and the sharp-witted Archdeacon of Brecon, each of whom claimed the right of presentation; reciprocal excommunications led to a tussle from which Giraldus came off best. Newtown greets the traveller from Kerry with vast red-brick edifices, the flannel factories and clothing warehouses of the Pryce-Jones firm. The broad and seemly thoroughfare leading down to the Severn bridge has on its east side a half-timbered *and thatched* inn, the "Chequers," reputed to date from King John's reign; its pewter tankards are certainly venerable. Do not look for the church: it is, at least externally, frankly hideous. Its windows are filled with glass of "Reckitt's blue" shade—the old tower, of the regular Border type, stands low by the river.

The shorter Kerry-Montgomery route runs between the foothills of Clun Forest and an isolated crescent of upland, Cefn-y-Coed, on one peak of which (Town Hill), within a clump of pines crowning an earthwork circle, stands a local War Memorial; whosoever chose this site displayed imagination and unconventionality; from it is the magnificent circular prospect, of which part of the northward expanse is seen in the illustration in the Introduction (5). The little town of Montgomery—well, to use modern advertising jargon, Montgomery is "different." It is hard to say where this quality lies; perhaps partly in its general lay-out, of which the churchyard provides an enlightening view. The central square gives one satisfaction, though it contains no really "picturesque" buildings.

The church is worth inspecting for its splendid rood screen, its timber-framed barrel roofs and its Herbert monuments, which include one to the first Lord Herbert of Cherbury's father. Lymore Hall, which stood a bowshot from the town, was one of the most superbly beautiful half-timbered mansions in the whole Border, now tragically demolished.

The original Montgomery Castle (5) was set up on its dizzy height by Roger de Montgomery soon after the Conquest and

destroyed by a Welsh force during the reign of Rufus. The
scanty ruins are those of a stronger castle-dwelling that dates
from Henry III's time and was badly damaged in the Civil
War, and afterwards neglected by the Herbert owners as being
too uncomfortable and inaccessible to reside in.

On the very straight road from Montgomery to Chirbury
notice "Salop" for *Shrewsbury* on the milestones. Chirbury,
head of a small marcher lordship, was named after a camp,
Caer Bre, that overlooks Marrington Dingle, a narrow glen
watered by the Camlad. The Dingle skirts the grounds of half-
timbered Marrington Hall (not shown). The parish church
has an attractive Early English doorway: the chief inn contains some good period furniture.

The remainder of the homeward route, which proceeds by
way of Church Stoke, Lydham (near Bishop's Castle), Eaton
and Plowden (p. 82), offers another series of charming views
in which the browns and greens of arable and pasture and
woodland are set off by the grey of rocky hillsides and the
purple of distant moors. On the first stretch the eyes are held
by dissolving views of Corndon Hill, which from one point
shows the outline of a flawless cone. The curious little rugged
hill beyond it also looks tempting. Between Church Stoke and
Lydham you may gaze westward along the protracted edge
of Clun Forest and Kerry Hill, or catch a glimpse northwards
of a fin-like outcrop of rock on the Stiperstones. The road
between the end of the Longmynd and Craven Arms has
been previously described.

SHIPTON HALL, CORVE DALE
(Drawn by Sydney R. Jones)

88 STOKESAY CASTLE AND CHURCH, SHOWING THE GREAT
HALL AND KEEP

89 AYMESTREY VILLAGE, IN THE LUGG VALLEY, BACKED BY THE
CROFT AMBREY HEIGHTS

90   THE HEATH CHAPEL, AN UNTOUCHED NORMAN BUILDING
ABOVE CORVE DALE

91   THE CHURCH, LYDBURY NORTH, SHROPSHIRE

CHAPTER VIII

THE SHROPSHIRE HIGHLANDS AND ADJACENT PARTS OF WALES. NORTHERN SECTION: CHURCH STRETTON, WELSH-POOL, LLANRHAIADR-YN-MOCHNANT AND SHREWSBURY DISTRICTS

THE natural centre for rambles over and rides round about the more spectacular Shropshire Highlands is Church Stretton, which like the other Strettons owes the second part of its name to the Roman road from *Bravonium* (Leintwardine) to *Viroconium* (Wroxeter), though the actual *strata via* coincides with the modern Shrewsbury road only between Marshbrook and Little Stretton. Travelling from the south by the latter road one becomes conscious of a sudden change in the quality of the scenery on reaching Marshbrook: though you are still in England, your surroundings are typically Welsh. Thereafter for some six miles the heather-clad slope of the Longmynd, scored by numerous "hollows," "batches," and "gutters," rises steeply on left: on the east side a succession of sudden peaks, a mountain range in miniature, diverts one's gaze. The names of the chief peaks are Ragleth Hill, the southernmost; Hazler and Hope Bowdler Hills, facing Church Stretton; Caer Caradoc, the highest (1506 ft.); and the Lawley, opposite the north end of the Longmynd. Caer Caradoc, a rugged cone (94) is crowned by a large oval earthwork with double defences. The Lawley (94) sends out a long spur, Hoar Edge, which merges northwards in Acton Burnell Park. Scattered woods mantle the flanks of some of these hills, and in combes on their eastern side are the villages of Hope Bowdler and Cardington, and the splendid mansion of Plashe (*i.e.* Plâs?), Elizabethan for the most part, built of red brick, and showing a wealth of mullioned windows and gabled walls and marvellous groups of twisted chimneys; an exotic note is added by modern octagonal towers with ogee roofs which are to disappear.

Acton Burnell (see above) has a beautiful Early English church (the oddly-placed tower is modern), cruciform in plan, containing the tomb and splendid brass of Nicholas Burnell (1382) and two monuments to Lees of Langley Hall (the famous Confederate general, Robert E. Lee, was a scion of this stock). The building has certain eccentrically-placed windows that have greatly puzzled antiquarians. Its erection is attributed to Robert Burnell, Bishop of Bath and Wells, Edward I's Chancellor and valued adviser. It was he that in 1283 got leave to crenellate the manor-house, the ruined shell of which, a long rectangle of walls with a square tower at each corner, stands in Acton Burnell Park near fragments of an earlier hall. It was to Acton Burnell Castle, one or other of these buildings, that Edward I's first *complete* Parliament was transferred from Shrewsbury to pass the *Statutum de Mercatoribus* (1283). The modern Hall is a large classical building. East of the park lies the site of Langley Hall, of which the beautiful Elizabethan gatehouse remains: Langley Chapel retains Commonwealth-period furniture—a canopied reader's pew, and rails ranged around a Communion Table after the fashion of the primitive Christians.

The northward road from Acton Burnell skirts the grounds of Pitchford Hall, one of the largest and most elaborate examples of half-timbered work in England, beyond which a left turn leads to Condover. The prominent wooded peak seen eastward is the Wrekin, whose name is a local symbol and rallying-cry. Condover Hall is a stately Elizabethan mansion of stone set off by gardens exhibiting curious examples of the art of topiary. It was built by that Judge Owen whom a remnant of the "red-haired banditti of Dinas Mawddwy" did to death at lonely Bwlch-y-Fedwen[1]; there are monuments to Owens and their collateral descendants the Cholmondeleys in the Carolean parish church. The Cholmondeley monuments, mid-Victorian (one is by G. F. Watts), are sometimes admired. Of this family was Mary Cholmondeley, whose *Red Pottage* shattered an unhealthy convention by its lifelike portrait of a strait-laced parson who was also a domestic tyrant and a nasty sadist. At the other end of the "range," on a southern slope of Ragleth Hill, is another splendid Tudor mansion of stone—Acton Scott Hall, best approached from Marshbrook.

Church Stretton offers a wide variety also of excursions over its mountainous western hinterland. The loveliest of the Longmynd ravines (93) are Ashes Hollow and the much-photographed Cardingmill Valley. The former, near Little

[1] Between Garthbeibio (Mont.) and Dinas Mawddwy. The scene of the crime is still called Llidiart-y-Barwn (The Baron's Gate).

92   THE ANCIENT WAY ACROSS THE LONGMYND LOOKING TO THE STRETTON HILLS

94 CAER CARADOC AND THE LAWLEY SEEN ACROSS STRETTON DALE FROM THE COMBES OF THE LONGMYND

95　THE SEVERN AT POOL QUAY, BELOW THE LONG MOUNTAIN

96　THE HAMLET OF BRIDGES IN THE LONGMYND

Stretton, is overlooked by the earthworks—the sole remains —of Brockhurst Castle, where Roman fort was replaced by moated Saxon *burh*, and this in turn by Norman stronghold. South of Little Stretton is Minton, where the outlines and general arrangement of a Saxon village may be studied. The Cardingmill Valley, near Church Stretton, is the winding gorge of a rock-strewn stream that may be traced almost to the summit-ridge, near which it forms the single fall of Light Spout. On one of the high bluffs north of the valley is Bodbury Ring, an earthwork fort; beyond it is—a golf course!

Church Stretton, lying some 600 ft. above sea-level, is a recognized health resort; modern hotels and opulent-looking villas have largely replaced its ancient buildings and extended its area. It manufactures mineral waters of deservedly high repute. The Perpendicular church tower is a prominent landmark. The tour I am about to sketch—possible in its entirety only for the strenuous cyclist or capable equestrian—will reveal the topography of the Shropshire highlands to the west and north-west. This follows first a steep but motorable road starting near the church, which after offering views down into the Cardingmill Valley bears away from it and mounts to the broad summit-ridge of the Longmynd. Soon it traverses a heathery hollow and arrives at a signpost, where it crosses the Portway (92). Our route lies forward, to Ratlinghope (pronounced "Ratchup"); but first you should wade through whinberry bushes and heather to the actual summit (1696 ft.: slightly south of the Medlicott track). The first time I found the summit it was occupied by a young couple and their fox-terrier, seated there with profiles outlined like cameos against a cirrused sky, and all three studying topography. The moving finger of the man was followed round by the eyes of the girl and the dog's muzzle as he pointed first to the fantastic Stiperstones close by, then in turn to Corndon's peak, the long edge of Clun Forest and Kerry Hill, the bulk of Radnor Forest, and dimly, blue on the horizon, the Black Mountains.

On the way down to Ratlinghope—rough, steep and gated —pause now and then for retrospective views. Woods sprawl aslant on the hillside against a background of rising moorland; below are cattle pastures cloven by the East Onny; the forward skyline is rendered strangely irregular by the excrescences— outcrops of quartz that variously resemble castle ruins or huge fins or the teeth of a mastodon or a cross-cut saw—projecting from the Stiperstones hog's-back. Nearing Ratlinghope, turn

M

left and after a time right; you will thus reach a main (Shrews-bury-Bishop's Castle) road just after crossing the East Onny beside a group of substantial houses and farm-buildings called appropriately Bridges (96). Immediately opposite is a gate admitting to a grassy, rutted track pointing straight at the Stiperstones summit.

For a more sequestered route across the Longmynd, adventurous ramblers may start from Leebotwood, follow the road to Woolstaston—a former rector of which once on his way back from Ratlinghope spent a terrible night and day in the snow on Longmynd—and beyond Woolstaston Hall[1] continue along a very tortuous track via Betchcott and Picklescott, reaching the Shrewsbury road a long mile north of Bridges.

The next stage can only be performed on foot, though a cycle will be useful—perhaps necessary—when you reach the valley beyond the Stiperstones. Those who use a car to cross the Longmynd can turn south at Bridges and make their way to Craven Arms via Wentnor, a pretty village set off by a hill crowned with a pine-clump; or, better, follow the main road north, amid wild and lonely country, over a high pass (1032 ft.), beyond which it descends past Church Pulverbatch and the park of Longden Manor to Shrewsbury; or start northward but turn off through Church Pulverbatch and get back to Stretton via Stapleton, where the double church has fine Early English lancets contrasting with early Norman work.

Trampers, with or without cycles, will follow the Stiperstone track mentioned above. When approaching a tree-girt farmhouse, avoid a right turn; beyond the house go straight forward, and when the track becomes blurred on the open moor, make for a sort of bare saddle where the summit-ridge is free of the protruding rocks. Arrived there you are rewarded with a view towards Wales that takes in Corndon and Stapeley Hills, the Long Mountain and the Breiddens, and the distant Berwyns; eastward you are faced with the interminable crest of the Longmynd. From your saddle you can walk along the ridge in either direction to examine some of the strange Ordovician outcrops. To south lies the summit (1731 ft.) and the huge mass of jagged rock called the Devil's Chair—the other "stiper-stones" being an apronful spilt by Old Nick. The best descent is by a grass track going south along the western side below the outcrops. Near some inhabited cottages

---

[1] "Hall" in titles of Shropshire houses has not necessarily a manorial-lordly implication, but often denotes a farmhouse.

97   THE BREIDDEN HILLS ABOVE THE SEVERN

99   IN BUTCHER ROW, SHREWSBURY

98   THE COUNCIL HOUSE GATEWAY, SHREWSBURY

you reach a metalled road that forks disconcertingly; the point to make for is the tall chimney of disused lead-works visible below. Having reached this with its unsightly slag-heaps and the few cottages that are Pennerley, go forward uphill to Shelve Church, and ignoring a track that leads to the tempt-ingly-named Squilver (87), climb again and then descend into another main road (A488). Solace is offered to the thirsty by an inn half a mile to right, near still-worked Roman gravel pits.

The western main road from Bishop's Castle leads north through the very charming Hope Valley to Shrewsbury via Minsterley and Pontesbury; southwards it goes under the lee of Corndon alongside the West Onny—step across which, and you are in Wales—to the Lydham cross-roads (p. 86).

The longish hill seen north of Corndon as you descend from Shelve is Stapeley Hill, on which are two well-preserved stone circles, Mitchell's Fold on the southern slope, Hoarstone Circle on the northern. To approach Mitchell's Fold in mist through which Corndon looms dimly ahead gives one a complete sense of desolation. This circle is associated with the legend of a magical and ill-tempered cow—a pendant to the legend of the giant bull which got into the church at Hyssing-ton (south of Corndon) and nearly burst its walls by most impiously inflating itself to capacity.

From Minsterley one may cross the wide valley of the little Rea Brook to Westbury or Brockton, in order to view Caus Castle site; or pass through Westbury to Middleton, for the ascent of the Breiddens (97). Westbury and Brockton are linked by a lane that traverses foothills of the Long Mountain; on a hill-spur south of this lane, about a mile from the West-bury end, are the bulky grass-grown mounds and ridges and scanty scraps of masonry that now represent the once mighty Caus Castle, the Border fortress of the powerful Corbets. The castle, a rectangle of curtain walls with angle towers and, at the east end, on a high mound that still remains, a massive keep, covered six acres, and below the hill-spur was a small town peopled by Corbet retainers; all have vanished "like the baseless fabric of a vision." Another Corbet property was the prettily half-timbered Marche Hall, north-west of Westbury: from the western side of Marche Park a lane goes westward to ascend the Long Mountain, and becomes a track that runs right along the summit-ridge and, after passing near the lonely little half-timbered church of Trelystan, descends to Forden, four miles north of Montgomery. From the ridge there are grand views, which include the Shropshire Highlands, the neighbouring Breiddens, the rolling Berwyns and a section of the Severn valley. The western (Welsh) slope of the Long Mountain, over the southern end of which spreads the wooded park of Leighton Hall, another property of the Shropshire Leightons of Plashe (p. 87), is seen to best advantage from the Welshpool neighbourhood, across the Severn (95).

An excellent road to Welshpool descends from Forden to Severn's bank, crosses the river by a bridge offering pleasant views in each direction, and after skirting a park that rises towards an impressive but not wholly attractive castle of red stone—Powis Castle; to the Welsh, Castell Coch (red castle) —enters the town which was anciently and still is locally called, without prefix, Pool.

The Celtic princes of Powys (roughly speaking, Montgomeryshire and north Radnorshire) were sitters on the fence, taking the Welsh or the Norman side as their interests dictated. We have seen how Gwenwynwyn attacked the unpleasant William de Braose at Painscastle. The oldest part of Powis Castle was built in Edward I's time by a gentleman of Shropshire named Charlton, whom that king had chosen as a suitable husband for Hawys, heiress of the last male descendant of Gwenwynwyn: she was no unwilling damsel dragged in tears to the altar, for it was at her own request that Edward had acted as matrimonial agent. The most prominent features of the castle are its huge embattled drum-towers, which rather dwarf the added Tudor mansion; other additions were made when the fortune of a "nabob" was poured into the Herbert coffers.[1]

Welshpool for the most part is spread with a happy irregularity of roofs and frontages along two parallel main streets and their divergent continuations. Half a dozen roads meet at Welshpool: of these B4391, which displays certain frontages of hoary antiquity, is worth following all the way to Llanrhaiadr-yn-Mochnant, on the southern fringe of the Berwyns, though if you are cycling its constant ups and downs will severely test muscles, wind and resolution: it crosses successively the valleys of the Vyrnwy, its tributary the Cain, and the Tanat. Two miles from Welshpool make a detour to Guilsfield church. This little-known building, dedicated to the Welsh saint Aelhaiarn, has marvellous roofs panelled after the fashion of a Roman *lacunar*, with floral bosses at the rib-crossings and painted masonic signs in the panel centres (100).

[1] In Charles I's reign the estate was bought by a William Herbert (descendant of the Yorkist Earl of Pembroke) who was made Earl of Powis (second creation).

101 THE YARD OF THE OLD POST OFFICE INN, SHREWSBURY

100 THE PANELLED CHANCEL ROOF, GUILSFIELD MONTGOMERYSHIRE

102   IN THE TANAT VALLEY, LOOKING NORTH-EAST

The conspicuous tower, Early English with a Decorated upper stage, displays a clock-face inscribed "Be diligent. Night cometh."

Approaching the Vyrnwy valley you cross the end of Broniarth Hill, near which the gallant and ill-rewarded Lollard leader, Sir John Oldcastle, after eluding Popish spies for four years, was finally recaptured (1417). From the next road-top, Bwlch-y-Cibau, the Berwyns are seen as lofty billowing moorlands descending in steep-sided spurs. Llanfyllin, in the ensuing valley, has pleasant outskirts, but its main street seems to wear a forbidding air of general disapproval. The name is *not* "Tlan-fillin," but (approximately) "Lhan-vuh-lhin." The bridge has attracted artists; we, however, do not cross the stream, but again climb heavenwards, reaching the road-summit at 1018 ft. The pleasantest approach to Llanrhaiadr is by way of Penybont-fawr, a hamlet smelling delightfully of wood-smoke, with a homely tavern where a cheerful stranger is welcomed. Llanrhaiadr-yn-Mochnant, which contains a modest but comfortable hotel, is chiefly visited for its proximity to Pistyll Rhaiadr, a waterfall 230 ft. high, broken only near its foot, but is also a good starting-point for tramps over the higher and wilder Berwyns. The most spectacular excursion from Llanrhaiadr is the trip up the Tanat valley to Llangynog, and thence literally upward by the (in places) dangerous road that crosses the Berwyns by a lofty pass (Milltir Cerrig, 1638 ft.) (10) and descends to Llandderfel, in the Dee valley, near Bala. The fine cul-de-sac valley which, between massive yet graceful hills, is ascended from Llangynog is that of the Eiarth (104), though it appears to be really the main stream: the name of Tanat itself is applied to the affluent flowing down a shorter impasse, that of Pennant (105), to the south. From beyond the pass-summit you obtain perhaps the finest of all distant views of the Snowdonian and Merionethshire mountains, each several peak being distinguishable by those who know their shapes; and eastwards the Berwyns undulate in heathery waves that culminate in Moel Sych and Cader Fronwen.

Within easy distance of Llanrhaiadr, Llanyblodwell has a wonderful half-timbered inn, the "Horseshoe," the licence of which has remained with the same family since Henry VIII's reign; here you may enjoy a dish of the Tanat trout. All this district saw stubborn fighting between Welsh and Angles and, later, between Welsh and Normans. Many of the hilltops hereabouts are crowned with "camps."

The Tanat valley between Penybont-fawr and Llanyblodwell, flat-floored between steep wooded walls often broken by glens, offers a continuous series of charming pictures (102, 103). From the valley road, at a point two miles east of Llangedwyn (the half-way village), a lane running northwards up a tributary dell crosses its stream at Pont Sycharth, near which, on the hither side of the bridge, are mounds marking the site of Sycharth, Owen Glyndwr's "royal palace" (his personal surname was taken from his other house at Glyndyfrdwy near Corwen). Beyond Sycharth bridge we join a hill-road that goes by way of Llansilin to a junction of Berwyn byways at Rhyd-y-croesau, then crossing an outer ridge at 1020 ft. descends past the park of Brogyntyn[1] into Oswestry. There is attractive scenery also in the Vyrnwy and Cain valleys near Llansantffraid-yn-Mechain, where the two rivers meet.

The Llandrinio-Shrewsbury highway, after crossing the Severn, skirts the northern end of the Breiddens (97); perhaps the best view of these startling peaks is obtained farther on, from Coedway, a hamlet on the actual border-line, with a pleasant anglers' inn. A track behind the inn leads to Braggington Hall, a Carolean brick-and-stone mansion with amusing spout-heads and gable finials and, within, a grand oak staircase. The main road presently crosses the extensive deer-park of Loton Park; three miles beyond, our road is joined by the Welshpool-Shrewsbury highway (A491). Middleton, half-way to Welshpool on the latter, is a starting-point for ascending the Breiddens (97). These are two peaks of volcanic origin, Moel-y-Golfa (1324 ft.) and Breidden Hill, with a slightly depressed saddle between them. The column on Breidden Hill commemorates Admiral Rodney's victories. A lane leading south from "Middletownhills" railway station (thus the name appears on the sign-board) brings one to Old Parr's Cottage, the dwelling of that Shropshire super-centenarian—described on a brass in Wollaston church as "The old, old, very old man, Thomas Parr"—who was born in Edward IV's reign and died, 153 years old, in that of Charles I. Unlike Tithonus he did not lose his zest for life: even after completing his first century he indulged not only in matrimonial but in less reputable sexual adventures. The story of his visit to London and interview with Charles I is well known. Dying at last in the gay metropolis, he was actually buried—perhaps owing to his feat of longevity—in Westminster

[1] A name that reappears—at Barmouth, too—as Porkington!

103   A WESTWARD VIEW IN THE TANAT VALLEY NEAR PENYBONTFAWR

LOOKING DOWN THE FIARTH VALLEY TOWARDS LLANGYNOG, MONTGOMERYSHIRE.

Abbey. His cottage, of timber-framed wattle-and-daub, must be nearly 500 years old.

Shrewsbury is entered by way of Frankwell and Welsh Bridge. The town is unusually rich in half-timbered buildings both simple and elaborate: a prolonged stroll about its centre will disclose not only single examples of merit, such as the Drapers' Hall, Ireland's Mansion, Owen's Mansion and Lloyd's House,[1] but whole alleys full, such as Grope Lane, Golden Cross Passage and Butcher Row (99): and other good specimens will be found in Mardol and Wyle Cop (each a part of the town's chief "throughway"), Frankwell and Dogpole: is there any town, except perhaps Norwich, that has a jollier collection of street-names?

Shrewsbury Castle, now the municipal headquarters, was founded by Roger of Montgomery, the Conqueror's Earl of Shrewsbury, founder also of Shrewsbury Abbey: the castle gateway is of his date, the drum towers are Edwardian. Near the castle are the *old* buildings of Shrewsbury School (founded in Edward VI's reign), now the Free Library and Museum: in the latter are numerous "finds" from *Viroconium* (Wroxeter). The Council House, lower down, was long the official dwelling of the President of the Council of the March: its gatehouse is a most satisfying piece of half-timbered work (98). Of ecclesiastical buildings three particularly may be mentioned. St. Mary's Church, which has a lofty spire giving distinction to all general views of Shrewsbury, is a perfect epitome of architectural styles, and contains much valuable ancient glass, especially in a Jesse window commemorating Hawys of Powys and her husband John de Charlton (see p. 92). The Abbey Church, which retains part of its original nave, has a large Perpendicular west window painted with heraldic shields of prominent families of the March, and is crowded with monuments brought here from demolished churches. St. Chad's Church, which replaces one of the same dedication that suddenly collapsed in ruins, sports a classical cupola: and —still more distinctive—an elliptical nave! It overlooks the Quarry, Shrewsbury's splendid public park, which centres on an avenue of lime trees leading to Severn's bank. The present buildings of Shrewsbury School were erected in 1882–83 at Kingsland, on the opposite bank. Here I may mention that the educated and older local (as opposed to the "board-school" and B.B.C.) pronunciation of the town's name

[1] From the Tudor period down to the Regency, Shropshire county families had their town houses here, not in London.

is *Shrozebury*, not Shroozbury[1]; and that "Salop," a Norman mispronunciation of the first syllable of the Anglian *Scrobbesbyrig*, was originally a name of the town, not of the shire: the title "proud Salopians" was first applied to those towns-folk who in 1642 rejected a reward proferred to them by Charles I for their loyalty.

It is impossible in these pages to give even a brief outline of a town's history so crowded with events as that of Shrewsbury. Certain points specially connected with Border history may be mentioned. *Pengwern* (alder hill) was the old Celtic name for this bluff within a loop of Severn; and it was to Pengwern that the Romanized Brythons retreated after the destruction of Wroxeter (584) by Ceawlin of Wessex. Two centuries elapsed before it was conquered by Offa and became a Mercian town. Roger of Montgomery, the Norman earl, was often harassed by Wild Eadric, last Anglian earl of Scrobbesbyrig, who made alliance with Welsh princes, formerly his enemies, and also gave sore trouble to Fitz-Osborn at Hereford. In 1215 Llewelyn the Great actually took the town after a siege, but the Red Dragon was driven out within a year; and the advance of Glyndwr's allies minus Glyndwr was more alarming than dangerous. Yet Shrewsbury still retains a not negligible Welsh population and a half-Welsh atmosphere.

Between the Cromwellian and Victorian periods western Shropshire was celebrated (or notorious) for its parish wakes or pleasure fairs, the attractions of which generally included the performance of some traditional play: *St. George and the Fiery Dragon* was a favourite. Bottom and his "hempen home-spuns" might have been Shropshire yokels. Drink flowed copiously at these feasts, and revellers often had to cross one of the ridges to reach their beds; if on summer nights they were "overcome" on the way, perhaps they might merely see visions like Eadric's phantom riders on the Stiperstones, but when a deep shroud of snow had turned the moorland heights into trackless indeterminate wastes, such journeys often ended in death. A Stretton wake held every St. Andrew's Day was long known as Deadman's Fair.

---

[1] In old documents it is often spelt *Shrowsbury*: cf. "show" and "shew."

105 LOOKING UP AT THE PENNANT VALLEY FROM ABOVE
LLANGYNOG, MONTGOMERYSHIRE

106 GREEN HILL AND OAK HILL ON THE STIPERSTONES RANGE

CHAPTER IX

CLWYDIAN HILLS AND VALE OF CLWYD: WREXHAM, MAELOR SAESNEG AND OSWESTRY: THE CEIRIOG VALLEY AND THE BERWYNS

IN the preceding chapter Oswestry, the northernmost point touched, was approached from the south: in this chapter I propose to work down to it from near the north end of Wat's Dyke. The northern section of the actual borderline bisects the Dee estuary and the canalized channel of the Dee, and comes within sight of Chester walls; then makes a sweep westward and returns to the Dee along the Pulford Brook, so that a good stretch of land—including Eaton Hall and its demesne—on what one would expect to be the Welsh side of the Dee is actually in Cheshire. Above the Pulford Brook the Dee separates Cheshire from Denbighshire for a space; then the intrusive Maelor Saesneg, the detached part of Flintshire, comes in and pushes the English-Welsh boundary out towards Malpas (Cheshire) and Whitchurch (Salop); but near the latter turns back, passes to north of Ellesmere and meets the Dee again at Erbistock, near Overton; after a few miles it deserts the Dee for the Ceiriog, and between Chirk and Llanymynech waveringly traverses outer spurs and valleys of the Berwyns.

I confess to being puzzled by the question what to treat as the essential Borderland in the northern part of this region. On one side of the Dee estuary is the Wirral, thoroughly "Nordic," for Danes succeeded Angles there as settlers. The Flintshire shore and the head of the estuary are uglified by a succession of grubby industrial towns such as Holywell, Bagillt, Glint, Connah's Quay, Queensferry and Hawarden, interspersed with vast isolated factories. The industrialized area extends southwards also to include Buckley, Wrexham and Ruabon and even encroaches on the sacred Vale of Llangollen at Cefn, Trevor and Acrefair. The devastation (speaking scenically) of this region is due not only to the presence of a large coalfield but to the occurrence of lead and other minerals in Halkin Mountain and the utilization of local kinds of stone in the manufacture of tiles and other coarse pottery, cement and chemicals.

On various grounds—and partly also, I admit, because of limits of space and personal predilections—I shall be arbitrary in choosing for my northern Borderland the Clwydian Hills, the upper part of the Vale of Clwyd, and the Llangollen district. Historically I have some excuse; the Clwydian Hills include many heights fortified by Cymric soldiers under direction of Brythonic chiefs against the Roman invader; later, the districts I have specified formed a chain of marcher lordships bordering on English counties.

The Clwydian Hills (4, 108) are a chain of heights of striking and varied outline, which look like mountains, especially when seen from the lower moors across the level Vale, though their culminating point, Moel Fammau, is under 2000 ft. high. Like the similar but lower hills about Church Stretton, these hills are of the Silurian epoch; in form and colouring they contrast strongly with the typical limestone scenery of most of Flintshire. The chain is broken by two main gaps: through one run the road and the railway-line linking Chester with Denbigh via Mold; the other, which is loftier and lies seven miles to south, is traversed by the fine Mold-Ruthin highway. Both these roads pass through interesting and beautiful country beyond Mold.

Mold is now a busy meeting-place of radiating lines of traffic; besides the routes mentioned and roads to various towns on the estuary shore, a long road traversing much wild country runs hence to Corwen in the Dee valley by way of Llandegla (p. 103) and Bryn Eglwys (p. 103). Mold parish church is a spacious Perpendicular edifice, impressive but perhaps too regular for beauty. On Bailey Hill, to north of the town, the Norman Robert de Monte Alto built a large motte-and-bailey, later covered by a stone castle, but hardly a trace of either remains. Robert's successors, who shortened the territorial name to Montalt (hence, apparently, the town's name *Mold*; the Welsh name is Y Wyddgrug), were kept in a constant state of liveliness by Welsh hostility.

Green and white are the prevailing hues of the typical Flintshire landscape; the limestone frequently crops out in cliffs and slopes of naked rock, and elsewhere has but a thin coating of mountain grass; but the hills are broken by wooded dingles.

Beyond Caerwys the Wheeler valley breaches the Clwydian

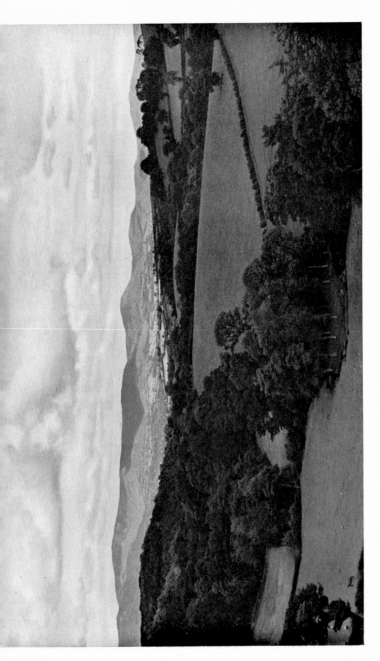

108 THE VALE OF CLWYD FROM SARON, NEAR DENBIGH

ROUNDING UP SHEEP IN THE REDWINGS FOR THE ANNUAL DIPPING AND SHEARING AT LARGEST

Hills: the scenery becomes more typically Welsh. On left the dizzy rock-strewn slope of Moel-y-Parc rises to its heathery crest; on right, as we emerge upon the Vale, Bodfari church, with its striped slate roof, is conspicuous below the camp-crowned Moel-y-Gaer. Moel-y-Parc has no entrenchment on its summit, but its neighbour Pen-y-cloddiau is crowned with a large elliptical earth-fortress of steep dykes and trenches, and other peaks southwards are similarly guarded. The Roman road from *Deva* (Chester) to *Conorium* (Caerhûn in the Conway valley) crossed the hills some miles north of this gap: it is not Bod*fari* but St. Asaph Palace that occupies the site of the Roman *Verae*. In a mile from Bodfari the road crosses the Clwyd, here already wide and gently-flowing: notice on left the grounds of Pont Ruffydd, a mansion still held by a Griffith. Crossing the Vale's level floor we are soon ascending that long, long street of Denbigh (114) which ends near the ruins of de Lacy's castle—but here I am encroaching on others' territory.

A far superior initial view of the Vale is enjoyed from the Mold-Ruthin road, which starts by climbing over a gap in a limestone ridge and descending into the Alun valley. The river is crossed close to the Loggerheads Inn, opposite which is the beginning of "The Leet," a path along a shelf of a limestone cliff above the stream; this is beloved of picnic parties, which usually halt at caves about a mile along it, but it may be followed to a road that leads to Cilcain, where the church has a wonderful roof, partly hammerbeam, purveyed from Basingwerk Abbey. From the "Loggerheads" our road bends southward up the Alun valley, but beyond Llanfeures bears away from it to ascend a high pass (944 ft.) through the Clwydians. A branch road leads up the Alun valley, which (though in Denbighshire) here displays the white-and-green of Flintshire, through Llanarmon-yn-lâl to Llandegla (p. 103). The suffix *yn-lâl* denotes that the parish was part of the marcher lordship of Yale.

At the pass-summit you have on left a wooded ridge and ravine across which appears the flank of Moel Gyw, down which a plantation of conifers cuts a sharp line. On right are heath-clad slopes that neighbour the steep-sided, camp-crowned Moel-Fenlli. A turn in the road over another ravine brings you to a point whence you can survey the richly-timbered Vale. From here its floor appears as a chess-board of browns and greens broken by spreading woods and the spacious parks of its numerous gentlemen's seats and lesser country houses, and dotted with frequent villages. Across the Vale, tier upon tier, are the colourful ridges of the Hiraethog, a moorland which extends unbroken to the Conway valley. The Hiraethog, like the Clwydians, is of Silurian age; the floor of the Vale is of the Triassic New Red Sandstone, but between the sandstone and the Silurian shales runs, on either side of the Vale, a narrow outcrop of limestone forming lower hills that show the usual features of limestone scenery—terraced cliffs, caves and fissures, deep gorges and patches of "clints."

Near the foot of the pass the road makes a very nasty hairpin bend. Beyond the "Griffin" and turnings to Llanrhydd and Llanhedr—which both have the suffix Dyffryn-Clwyd, indicating that they belonged to that marcher lordship—you pass the modern (and ugly) buildings of Ruthin's ancient grammar-school, descend between red banks and climb again steeply to Ruthin's market-square. Seen from a moderate distance, Ruthin is truly picturesque—far more so than most Welsh towns. If you ignore post-War outcrops it has the air of a still mediæval town. Its houses cluster thickly on the slopes of the miniature plateau occupied by church, market-square and castle. Red is the prevailing note, though there is a sprinkling of the magpie colours; the *comble* of the picture is the dignified though late-Victorian broach spire of the church. Beautiful ancient houses, some disguised by shop fronts, remain in Market Square, the Clwyd Streets, and Record Street. Near the castle an echoing passage leads to a raised walk that skirts ancient walls and looks down on a mediæval lord's mill beside the Clwyd.

Ramshackle ruins adjoining the Victorian Gothic Ruthin Castle represent the ancient castle of Grey de Ruthyn, Glyn Glyndwr's detested foe, who held the marcher lordship of fair Dyffryn Clwyd. Glyndwr acted quite in character when, one market day in 1400, he frightened the Welsh stall-keepers and chafferers by setting fire to the town, but wholly failed to take his English enemy's castle. Ruthin church, originally monastic but made collegiate by one of the Greys, has over the north aisle (the original nave) a magnificent carved and panelled *lacunar* roof, presented by Henry VII. The incumbent is known as The Warden, from his nominal connexion with a Hospital founded, like the grammar-school, by Gabriel Goodman, a Ruthin worthy who in Elizabeth's time became Dean of Westminster.

The easiest route for the ascent of Moel Fenlli and Moel

Fammau follows the Mold road to the dark entry of a lane turning off to left a short distance above the "Griffin" (p. 102). The lane merges into a rough track (the *old* Mold road) which mounts to a pass, Bwlch Pen Barras, between the two peaks. Just below the limit of cultivation on the near slope of Moel Fenlli is a "half-way" cottage; from its garden you look across the Vale to the billowy Hiraethog and see, rising beyond it like lofty islands, powder-blue in the distance, four great mountain-massifs. The most northerly, far more extensive than the others, comprises the three great Snowdonian groups —Snowdon itself, distinguishable among its satellite peaks by its sharp summit; the Glyders and Tryfan; and the smooth, bulky Carnedds. Southward, after a wide interval, comes Arenig, near Bala; the southernmost of the four massifs is formed by the twin peaks Aran Mawddwy and Aran Benllyn, at the head of Bala Lake; between and beyond Arenig and the Arans, Cader Idris appears.

Now, if you wish to see what an awkward job it must have been to attack hilltop entrenchments, clamber up to the summit of Moel Fenlli: the slope is steep, the heather waist-high, and the dimensions of the *valla* and *fossæ* amazing. Moel Fammau summit is gained by a green road ascending from the *bwlch* by an easy gradient. From the summit, near which is a strange little copse of wind-stunted trees, you get an extension of the westward view described above: eastwards you look across the Dee, the Wirral and the Mersey to the smoke-pall that indicates Liverpool.

Two roads lead from Ruthin up the Vale: one, the Wrexham road, goes off from the Mold road beyond the railway-bridge, and in two miles brings you into Llanfair-Dyffryn-Clwyd (see p. 102), offering *en route* continuous views of the Clwydians. The other, which continues Castle Street, is the Corwen Road; it skirts the foot of Coed Marchan, a fir-crowned limestone ridge, and in two miles closely approaches the Clwyd at Eyarth Bridge (see below); then bears westward and for several miles it ascends the upper valley of the Clwyd. This looks paradoxical, for the obvious Vale of Clwyd continues beyond Llanfair in the same alignment as before; but this continuation is actually watered by a tributary, the Hespyn. The Corwen and Wrexham roads are linked by a byway that crosses Eyarth Bridge, mounts a red-banked hill, and enters the village close to the "White Horse" inn, a hostelry of some merit adjacent to the church gates. If you take up a position by a field-gate fifty yards from and facing the inn's front door

—it is near a row of miniature Victorian villas facing a side-road that goes downhill—you may identify the nearer Clwydian peaks: Moel Fammau and its neighbour Fenlli you have already met; then, after a gap marking the Mold road, come in succession the rounded cone of Moel Gyw; the broad, flat-topped and clearly purple Moel Llech; Moel-y-Plas, which throws out two bold spurs towards the Vale; Moel-y-Waun, with a wavy top (flippant youngsters call it the Curlicue); and, as termination, the bold-profiled Moel-yr-Acar. Well to right of the last-named you will see a pair of rounded summits, looking down the Vale over the lower Cricor moors: one draws comfort from the presence of such serene sentinels. They are Moel-y-Gamelin and Moel Morfydd, peaks of Llantysilio Mountain, which lies between the upper Alun valley and the Dee gorge above Llangollen: we are soon to be more intimate with one of them.

From the lodge-gates of Eyarth, near Eyarth Bridge, you may—after asking for permission and directions at the lodge —walk a little way up the drive and beyond a bridge turn to right along a path that ascends through woods parallel with the Clwyd, which here runs through a lovely cliff-walled gorge, haunt of dipper and grey wagtail: or if you do not mind wading now and then, you can ascend beside the river, here a proper mountain stream, to the head of the gorge; you emerge near the foot of Eyarth Rocks, a terraced series of limestone cliffs, easily surmounted: from the summit-plateau, which is paved with clints, you have perhaps the best view of the head of the Vale. "Clints" are large patches of naked lime-stone scored by deep fissures beloved of ferns—maidenhair, hartstongue and polypody. Crossing the plateau to a gated farmyard you may there be set on a hilly path leading eventu-ally to a stony lane that is a genuine mediæval road: turn along this to left, and you are soon inhaling the scent of the pine-needles you trample as you skirt the garden wall of Llanfair Vicarage.

Llanfair church is constructed on a plan peculiar to the Vale of Clwyd and one or two neighbouring districts. Churches of this "Vale-of-Clwyd" type consist of two structural naves side by side: one nave has, as a rule, a west tower, and the east end of either aisle forms the chancel. Here the north aisle has both tower and chancel. Points to notice are ancient glass arranged kaleidoscope fashion in a south window, and a burial inscrip-tion on the west wall which include the unusual phrase *mortuus est in cantu galli*, "he died at cock-crow."

110 LOOKING TO THE EGLWYSEG RANGE FROM THE HORSESHOE PASS, NEAR LLANGOLLEN

III GATHERING STORM OVER THE MAIN RIDGE OF THE BERWYNS

Leaving Llanfair D.C. (as it is familiarly called), the Wrexham road undulates to the head of the Vale, passing near halfway the gate of a long drive leading to the lovely though unfinished Elizabethan mansion of Llwyn Ynn and the curious little Jesus Chapel, a chapel-of-ease built and endowed by a native of this parish (still Llanfair, which is of unusual extent) who became head verger of Westminster Abbey. The road now approaches the lower end of Nant-y-Garth Pass, the tortuous gorge of a little stream that flows by the road, perhaps the most beautiful miniature pass in Wales: it is barely three miles long, but every turn discloses some unexpected attraction. The containing walls, sometimes wooded slopes, sometimes open moor, are lofty, and at half-way there is a perfectly shaped "plum-pudding" hill, with gorse bushes to represent sultanas.

Near the top of the pass you see on left a conspicuous motte, Tomen-yr-adwy; beyond it on right the Llangollen road turns off, but this commendable route—it includes the "Horseshoe Pass"—may as well be joined from the "Crown," Llandegla's chief inn, which lies a straight mile onward. The "Crown" once earned distinction by providing afternoon tea for Mr. and Mrs. Gladstone, who were touring this countryside in a barouche: in Victorian days, for some inscrutable reason, the Welsh peasantry reverenced the High-Churchy W. E. Gladstone as one Person of a triune Deity of which the other two Persons were Queen Victoria and "S'r-Wattkin" (the reigning Williams-Wynn). The long hog's-back to south, cairned and heather-purple, is Cyrn-y-Brain; the Wrexham road continues past it over open moorlands but after a few miles traverses a string of mining villages. Let us therefore choose the Llangollen way, which soon crosses the upper Alun valley and a road for Bryn Eglwys and Corwen that passes the now sequestered mansion of the Yale lordship—Plas-yn-Iâl, home of a Pilgrim Father whose son, Elihu Yale, helped to found the great American University named after him. Soon Cyrn-y-Brain becomes obtrusive on left, Llantysilio Mountain, foreshortened, on right; the gradient stiffens; we cross the actual *col* (Bwlch Rhiw'r Ychain), but the road-summit (1353 ft.) is round a bend; arrived there, you see your road making a prodigious hairpin and running shelf-wise along the opposite hollow before it disappears round another corner. To left of the latter, over a wooded hill, loom the Eglwyseg Rocks (107), terraced limestone cliffs of a strange pinkish hue. At the head of the loop, where waste-heaps of a slate-quarry make giants' slides, you are near the summit of Moel-y-Gamelin (p. 102).

The "Horseshoe" is followed by a coasting run down a hill-flank above a stream. Approaching more level ground look out on left for Eliseg's Pillar and, soon afterwards, Valle Crucis Abbey. The Pillar, a cross now headless, was formed from a Roman column: this was the *crux* that gave a name to the valley and the abbey. It was first set up by Concenn, a prince of Powys, in honour of his great-grandfather Eliseg, who fell at that battle of Chester (603) where Angles under Aethelfrith defeated Welsh under Eliseg's son Brochmael. Valle Crucis Abbey, which among ecclesiastical ruins has no rival in the Borderland save Tintern, and has not, like Tintern, been prettified by the Office of Works, was founded in 1200 for Cistercians by another prince of Powys, Madoc ap Griffith Maelor, whose palace stood in what is now Wynnstay Park. The setting of the abbey ruins, which includes fish-ponds that mirror them, approaches perfection: the east front with its tiers of lancets, the west front with its gable rose-window, and the vaulted chapter-house, illustrate both the development and the beauty of the Early English style. Our road skirts a long reach of the Dee before crossing it by a fourteenth-century bridge and entering Llangollen.

The fame of Llangollen is due less to its own charm than to that of its exquisite surroundings—the narrow wooded gorge threaded by the Dee above the town and the steep hills that girdle it about, Dinas Bran on north crowned by castle ruins, Pen-y-coed opposite and to south-west Moel-y-Geraint, a natural belvedere. As general background you have on one side Llantysilio Mountain and the spectacular Eglwyseg Rocks, on the other the loftier Berwyns. Plas Newydd, notorious as the home of the more than slightly ridiculous "Ladies of Llangollen"—though they affected Welsh top-hats, one was English, the other Irish; both would have derived benefit from psychoanalysis — has lost much of the old carved oak with which, vicariously bought or stolen from churches and ancient houses, they overloaded the interior; the exterior is still excessively "half-timbered." At holiday seasons not only is the town crowded, but its main thoroughfare, being part of Telford's great Holyhead road, roars with a never-ceasing stream of traffic. Hereabouts the prudent angler still fishes from a coracle.

112 VIEW FROM NERQUIS MOUNTAIN, NEAR WREXHAM, ON THE FRINGES OF THE HILL COUNTRY

112. THE UPPER CEIRIOG VALLEY; LLANARMON DYFFRYN CEIRIOG, WITH THE BERWYNS AS

Climb up to Castell Dinas Bran and you will be able to gauge the ardency of the passion that inspired a poor Cymric poet to toil up this dizzy slope nightly in order to serenade, with his own compositions, the golden-tressed Brythonic heiress Myfanwy Vychan—who after all married a man of property. A lane no less steep, and painfully stony, links Llangollen direct with Llansantffraid-Glyn-Ceiriog ("Glyn" for short), but the road-route via Chirk and the lower Ceiriog valley (113) is more attractive. There is, however, a delightful way for walkers that starts by skirting Penycoed, climbs over a long spur of the Berwyns, traverses in succession a deep wood and the whole length of Chirk Castle deer-park, passing near the castle, and emerges into the Ceiriog valley road near Chirk. The main features of Chirk Castle, which consists of a large quadrangle of heavy red-sandstone walls, with massive angle drum-towers and on north a gateway, are of Edwardian date; but it was damaged during the Great Rebellion and has been much modernized. The main entrance-gates to the castle park (115), a *chef-d'œuvre* of artistic wrought-iron work, were designed and made about 1720 to the order of Sir Robert Myddleton by three local craftsmen, Robert Davies and two brothers called Roberts; the Emral Hall gates in Flintshire also are their work. Castle and grounds are open to the public on certain days weekly.

Travellers who prefer the road-route will find that below Llangollen the Dee valley broadens into green hedge-bordered water-meadows, showing an industrial smudge only on the farther side where it approaches the lowlands. This broader portion is crossed successively by two engineering master-pieces, Telford's Fron Cyssyllte Aqueduct, which carries a canal, and the Cefn railway viaduct. Similar but smaller con-structions, and also a lofty road-bridge, cross the Ceiriog near Chirk.

From the Llangollen-Chirk road, as you approach the Cefn viaduct, A540 branches off close to a house called Plas Offa (a finely preserved section of the Dyke traverses Chirk Castle Park), crosses the Dee by a bridge offering delightful views up stream, and runs through the smoke of Cefn to Ruabon. Conspicuous on right as you enter this town are the gates of Wynnstay Park, which admit favourites of Fortune to a mile-long avenue of noble trees. Wynnstay is the chief seat of the Williams-Wynns, a family which derives blood from several Welsh stocks and is distinguished for never having produced any man of more than local distinction except one respectable

o

politician who also was a dilettante of the arts, maintaining (as Lord Howard de Walden has done at Chirk Castle) a model theatre and band of amateur players at Wynnstay.

THE JACOBEAN STAIRCASE, HEATH HOUSE, CLUNGUNFORD
(Drawn by H. T. Timmins)

114 THE WAY OUT OF DENBIGH TOWN

115 THE EARLY EIGHTEENTH CENTURY GATES AT CHIRK CASTLE,
THE WORK OF THE ROBERTS BROTHERS

116   THE USK VALLEY HIGH ABOVE ABERGAVENNY, THE SUGAR LOAF IN DISTANCE

CHAPTER X

THE LOWER USK AND WYE VALLEYS:
THE LAND OF GWENT

THE southernmost part of the Borderland consists—strictly speaking—in those mining valleys of West Monmouthshire and East Glamorgan which trench the long southern slope of the moors terminated northwards by the escarpments of Mynydd Llangattwg and Mynydd Llangynidr, and bounded on two sides by the Usk Valley. This block of upland, which on the western side is bounded by Glyn Collwng and the valleys of the Taff and its tributary the Cynon, bears some general resemblance to the Black Mountains block; but its valleys are more numerous and closer together, its escarpment less bold, and the average height of its ridges 1000 ft. lower; and in place of red sandstone we here have the Carboniferous Limestone. Here are no haunts of Pan and Apollo, Corydon and Phyllis; Vulcan and Plutus are the local gods, even though their votaries sometimes shiver with empty pockets: perpetual tokens of their power are seen in the blackened and ravaged valleys of the Afon Llwyd, Ebbw, Sirhowy, Rhymney, Bargoed, Taff and Rhondda.

The official English-Welsh boundary climbs from the Grwyne Fawr over a corner of the Sugar Loaf, runs a couple of miles along the Usk, zigzags vaguely over hills south of the Clydach and over Mynydd Llangynidr, and finally coincides with the river Rhymney from source to mouth: thus Cardiff is only just in Wales. The real as opposed to the formal Anglo-Cymric Border—speaking quite roughly—bisects the Monmouthshire lowland, the country betwixt Usk and Wye: the eastern part of Monmouthshire is either English or thoroughly Anglicized. For several reasons I shall say nothing of the "Western Valleys" or of Usk's industrialized mouth.

Two excursions will, however, be suggested that approach or overlap the technical border-line. One of these routes follows the Abergavenny-Brecon road through Crickhowell to the first sharp angle on the hill approaching Bwlch, then turns left and crosses Llangynidr Bridge, which offers delightful views up and down the Usk and towards the enclosing hill-spurs. From Llangynidr—also accessible by a road from Crickhowell passing along the southern bank of the river—take the mountain road to Brynmawr, which starts by climbing the flank of a narrow wooded valley and, as the gradient stiffens, forms wide zigzags. At last you reach the broad plateau that links the Llangattwg and Llangynidr mountains, and can look back over the green and pleasant Usk valley to the unspoilt ridges of the Black Mountains (117), or forward towards the artificial desolation of the mining valleys—Elysium contrasted with Erebus. A few miles farther on you reach the main road that links the heads of the valleys, and turning along it eastwards can return to Abergavenny by the Clydach valley, which still can offer pleasant prospects here and there.

The second route includes the unfrequented side of the Beacons and the lovely Glyn Collwng, and involves a preliminary journey to Brecon. The whole length of the Abergavenny-Brecon road traverses scenes of rich beauty set off against looming moorlands that culminate westwards in the strange summits of the Brecon Beacons. The first portion, the "Vale of Crickhowell" leaves an impression of extraordinary opulence. Beyond Crickhowell you pass the grounds of Gwernvale (on right), once the property of an ancient family named Prodger (*ap Roger*), who lost it through foolish loyalty to King Charles "the Martyr." The house is curiously associated with another of those odd characters who have been attracted to the Black Mountains. Some forty years ago the then heir to the property became acquainted with a certain Frederic William Rolfe, author of certain works of strange charm, exotic and Yellow-Book-ish, of which the best-known was the euphuistic *Hadrian the Seventh*. Rolfe had been reared in a Protestant and bourgeois atmosphere, but had turned Romanist and tried—vainly, because of his unsatisfactory character—to take Orders in the Roman Church. He seems to have been partly deranged: one of his eccentricities was to assume the title of "Baron Corvo"—a pure invention. He so impressed the heir of Gwernvale by his hard-luck stories that the latter put him up and supplied his financial needs for two longish periods, one of over a year, and collaborated with him in a projected work: for recreation "Corvo" tramped the mountains in a purple velvet jacket. Then came a quarrel, provoked by Rolfe, in which the latter displayed a hitherto

117 THE USK VALLEY LOOKING TO CRICKHOWELL AND THE BLACK MOUNTAINS FROM THE
ABERGAVENNY ROAD

118   THE WYE VALLEY FROM NEWTON HILL, LOOKING TO STAUNTON, MONMOUTHSHIRE

119   LOOKING TO THE SUGAR LOAF HIGH ABOVE THE USK VALLEY FROM THE ABERGAVENNY-
BLAENAVON ROAD, MONMOUTHSHIRE

120 TINTERN ABBEY AND THE WYE VALLEY

hidden facet of his character: the upshot was that, though Rolfe threatened to "show up" the Gwernvale family by entering Crickhowell workhouse, velvet coat and all, the Gwernvale portal was thenceforward closed against him. It was just as well: his later history disclosed that it was not in religion only that he was a pervert.[1]

Beyond Gwernvale and the turning for Penygenffordd and Talgarth the Brecon road skirts in turn Glan Usk park and the wooded hill of Myarth, then climbs a zigzag to the high-perched village of Bwlch, whence the trio of peaks at the end of the Penalltmawr ridge is seen in retrospect to greatest advantage. We descend past Llansantffraid church, where gentle Vaughan "the Silurist" is commemorated by his tomb and a modern tablet. Approaching Brecon you have the Usk close below you for several miles, and the Beacons summits gradually assume a conical outline, though they can assume strange shapes and look like humped hogs'-backs ending northwards in abrupt scarps topped by pyramids. Glyn Collwng—a beautiful crescent-shaped valley—is comparable to the finest glens of the Scottish Highlands. At the extreme lower end a reservoir is in process of formation, but the upper portion is of quite unspoilt beauty. Glyn Collwng debouches into the Usk valley close to Talybont, whence you get back on to the main Abergavenny road a little west of Bwlch. If the mid Wye valley is your objective you can proceed from Bwlch via Llangorse Lake and Talgarth.

Abergavenny, the "gateway" to the more spectacular part of the Usk valley, is a true Border town, where Welsh and English residents and visitors intermingle in amity. Just as to-day it is a strategic point for holiday-makers with a passion for "going places and seeing things," so was it deemed strategic in the military sense by the Romans, who here planted their station of *Gobannium*, clumsily Latinizing the Celtic name of the little Gavenny stream; and by the Norman free-lance, Hamelin de Baladun, who built the first castle and also founded a priory. The importance of this narrow entry may be gauged from the erection of castles at Crickhowell, Tretower and Blaen-llyfni (near Bwlch) as an outer and (later) of the establishment of the Trilateral as an inner line of defence. The castle ruins, a gatehouse with portions of battered walls and towers, lie south of the town environed by a public garden. It was in this castle that William de Braose perpetrated the foulest of his unknightly deeds: seventy

[1] See *The Quest for Corvo*, by A. J. A. Symons, a biographical *tour de force*.

defenceless guests, Welsh warriors whom he had invited to a banquet under treacherous pretence of amity, were by his orders murdered at his own table. The priory church, a cruciform building situated near the beginning of the Monmouth road, has remarkable collections of monuments in the Lewis and Herbert Chapels (north and south choir aisles); one effigy is of timber. Notice in the Herbert Chapel the great timber figure of Jesse (126), which must once have represented the root of a colossal "tree of Jesse"; and the embellishments of the Roberts and Jones brasses, sweetly domestic in one case, horridly osteological in the other. The choir stalls, carved and canopied, have some interesting misericords.

The bustling main thoroughfare preserves only occasional traces of antiquity: to see what old Abergavenny was like— say, in the days when gentlemen wore perukes[1]—take a stroll up and around St. John's Street. The Bailey Park, off the Hereford Road, provides a good general view of the town and its surroundings. The four isolated peaks that are essential factors of Abergavenny's personality attract visitors whom strenuous mountain-walking would exhaust. Of the two to east, Skyrrid Fawr has been described (Chapter IV); Skyrrid Fach, the baby, is close to the G.W.R. station and is laid out as a pleasance for strolls; southwards it overlooks the park of Coldbrook House, earliest of the many Herbert demesnes in this shire.

The Blorenge (1834 ft.), which retains its cumbrous shape owing to its cap of millstone grit, is easily climbed from the Garnddyrys Inn on the *upper* road to Pontypool. The Sugar Loaf (1955 ft.)—whose formal style is Mynydd Pen-y-Fal (Peak-top Mountain)—descends southwards towards the town in three spurs separated by lovely wooded dingles. The central spur, Rholben, offers the easiest ascent. Like many other peaks of moderate height, the Sugar Loaf provides satisfying views. The most direct route to the Grwyne valleys is the old road that passes between Sugar Loaf's eastern spur (Deri) and the detached Bryn Aro and reaches the Grwyne Fawr valley at Fforest (p. 18).

Dear old William Coxe, whose discursive *Historical Tour of Monmouthshire* (1801) is at once a sedative and a liberal education in topographical method, describes in an inimitable passage—priceless I had almost called it—how he achieved the (to him) fatiguing ascent of the Sugar Loaf.

[1] Abergavenny was then an important wig-making centre.

121   THE WYE VALLEY BY HARDWICK CLIFFS, WITH THE SEVERN ESTUARY BEYOND

122   THE SUGAR LOAF MOUNTAIN FROM THE RIVER USK, NEAR ABERGAVENNY

"It was near six o'clock, and I hastened to join a party returning from the ruins of Llanthony Abbey. I partook of an elegant collation, provided by my friend Mr. Greene, which was spread on the banks of the Honddy: the wine, *interiore notâ Falerni*, was cooled in the limpid and murmuring stream; the evening was placid and serene, and I forgot the fatigues of the day in convivial intercourse and social conversation."

The direct Abergavenny-Monmouth road, which passes near White Castle, has been described in Chapter IV. A longer route goes by way of Raglan: the first portion of it is part of the main or lower Usk road (A471), which starts along the left bank of the river, passing Coldbrook, and in about five miles turns abruptly southwards and crosses to the right bank; the Raglan and Monmouth road continues forward. Some three miles beyond the road-junction we recross the river. Opposite Trostrey church, half hidden in trees above us, the river makes a wide loop, seen against a background of far-away moorland, with rich woods in the middle distance. Presently our road absorbs the "upper" Usk road (see below), and after running for a mile alongside a straight reach of the river we enter the town of Usk.

The upper (and pleasanter) Usk road leaves the Raglan road and exactly opposite the mock-Gothic portal of the drive to Clytha House. The latter is a Herbert property; the Raglan road cuts the park into two portions. An owner of the Jane-Austen period who caught the craze for artificial ruins and gazebos and temples of Diana punctuated these pleasant park-lands with such oddities, and some of them remain. One of them "Clytha Castle," an essay in castellar Gothic, overlooks the upper Usk road, which runs southwards along the left river bank—for the river has bent southwards too.

For the systematic exploration of the quadrilateral bounded by lines joining Abergavenny, Monmouth, Chepstow and Caerleon, no place is more conveniently situated than Usk, itself a fishing-centre for the river whose name it bears, an important mart for sales of farm stock, and a town with a long history illustrated by its castle and priory church: learned men have even identified it with the Roman *Burrium*, but the actual site is still to seek. What is more important to the way-farer is that Usk contains one of the most comfortable and intelligently conducted hotels in all the Border—the venerable "Three Salmons." It has an old interior modernized in the way of bathrooms and lighting; in season you are offered fresh

Usk trout for breakfast and a choice between Usk salmon and Severn salmon for dinner, the beds are soporific, and if you *do*—after salmon—remain wakeful you will find (*mirabile dictu*) a judicious selection of books in your bedroom. Expensive? Far from it: this is not a resort of *nouveaux riches* or the suburban genteel: most of the guests are engrossed in piscatorial achievements and technicalities. Then there is Patricia —but I will not expatiate on that paragon of parlourmaids. Usk Castle, perched on a low scarped hill, is approached from the town by a steep path. The ruins consist of a grass-floored quadrangle having on the east side the main gateway and a square keep, opposite these a large round tower, and on the north portions of the hall and dwelling-rooms.

Visitors to Usk interested in Roman Britain will, of course, make a pilgrimage to Caerleon; will gaze upon a large fragment of the city wall of *Isca Silurum*, walk round its skilfully excavated amphitheatre, and spend profitable hours in its well-docketed museum. The direct way to Caerleon is gained by crossing Usk Bridge: it travels southwards, partly coinciding with the Roman road, through a country of strange Silurian outcrops—low irregular hills and little cliffs, often well wooded—that occur in this part of Monmouthshire between the mountain limestone and the old red sandstone.

But if you travel southwards from Usk merely with a view to general study of the countryside, choose the lesser road, which leaves the town unobtrusively near the amusing old market house and proceeds along the eastern bank of the Usk: this is on more intimate terms with the river and takes you through a charmingly variegated countryside "remote from public haunt." The river goes gently rolling along below you with alternation of loop and short reach; fine old trees and groups of trees grace the water-meadows: there is noble secular timber, for instance, round about Llanbadoc.

Continuing our gentle road along the Usk bank: soon after parting with a skyward lane we skirt a long flank of Went Wood showing bits of cliffs, known as Kemeys Graig. The little church placed hereabouts between road and river is that of Kemeys Inferior; the name Kemeys is that of a notable local family. A mile beyond this church turn south, and at the next road-junction, by executing a rapid right and left, keep on southward: you will thus reach the Newport-Chepstow road opposite a conspicuous ancient mansion, tall and gaunt, perched on a hillside—Llangstone Court.

It would take a week to examine at all thoroughly all the

123 MONNOW BRIDGE, MONMOUTH, WITH ITS DEFENSIVE TOWER

124 CHEPSTOW CASTLE, ON THE WYE, MONMOUTHSHIRE

125   SWIFT'S HOUSE, GOODRICH, OF TYPICAL BORDER SOLIDITY

126   THE EFFIGY OF JESSE, DEPRIVED OF HIS TREE,
ABERGAVENNY PRIORY CHURCH

ancient buildings and other objects of interest that either lie
on or are easily reached from the main road between here and
Chepstow. Only the more notable of these can be mentioned
here. A topographical outline of the district is a necessary
preliminary. On the north of the road are foothills rising to
the great ridge of Went Wood, which is continued by Chepstow Park Wood and other eminences all the way to the Wye,
its actual termination being the Wynd-cliff. South of the road
are other low hills, but between these and the Bristol Channel
a band of alluvial flats, of an average width of three miles,
extends from the Usk mouth to Mathern near Chepstow. This
is the Caldicot Level: it is intersected by ditches known as
rhines—a term also found on Sedgmoor in Somerset—and the
seaboard is fretted by little creeks or *pills*. On the western side
of Usk mouth are similar flats—the Wentlloog Level—
extending to Cardiff.

We return to the main road: three miles beyond the Llan-
martin turn, the questing eye is caught by an abrupt hill on
right, crowned by a truly picturesque embattled house and,
behind it, a little church tower with pyramidal roof. The
house is Penhow Castle: besides crenellated walling and an
intact square tower there is a fragmentary Norman Keep in
the farmyard.

Caerwent, three miles onward, was the Roman *Venta
Silurum*, which after the establishment of *Isca* became a mart
and residential town. Systematic excavation has brought to
light foundations of town walls and gates, basilica, amphitheatre, temples and villas; even wells and water-pipes have
been unearthed. Filling-in has necessarily followed excavation, but in the village museum a detailed plan is displayed
and a large and representative collection of finds preserved.
The old Caerwent-Usk road (surely not Roman?) was the
skyward lane (p. 112): a southward continuation brings you
to Caldicot, where the church will interest ecclesiologists, and
within sight of Caldicot Castle—used now as a residence, but
shown to serious applicants. The splendid frontage of the castle
displays a reconditioned gatehouse with massive tower and a
stretch of wall pierced by traceried windows of a vanished hall.

Finally, the main road climbs through the suburb of Hardwick and passing under the ancient West Gate descends
Chepstow's main street towards the Wye Bridge, to left of
which stands the famous Chepstow Castle—the Striguil of the
Normans (124). Chepstow, to-day rather apt to be overrun
by trippers, has been a place of habitation since the days of the

P

Brythons. As its name shows, it was later held by the Saxons; the first Norman castle was built here by FitzOsborn of Hereford. When FitzOsborn's son earned disgrace and imprisonment the lordship of Striguil passed to the great family of de Clare, and one holder of the castle was Strongbow (Richard de Clare), who first established the English Pale in Ireland. Later, it passed successively, through marriages of various heiresses, to Marshalls, Bigods, Herberts[1] and Somersets: a Somerset, the Duke of Beaufort, owns it to-day.

Owing to its situation on a narrow ridge, which descends in a cliff to the Wye and less abruptly on the other side to "The Dell," the castle is of unusual plan. It consists of four courts, not concentric, but placed end to end. To left of the main gateway, which admits to the First Court, is the massive round tower, curiously "spurred," where Henry Marten, "regicide," Puritan and poet, suffered a long though not very close imprisonment: his inscribed tombstone may be seen in Chepstow church. The hall and other apartments are on the river side of the First Court. The Third Court incorporates the ancient keep. The Fourth Court is separated from the others by a trench and has a postern gate. Except for the keep the castle is mainly Edwardian. The greater part of the old town walls remains; they are generally obscured by other buildings, but may be studied near the castle and near the station. The parish church displays a Norman front of much beauty: the late addition of an incongruous tower was an error.

Returning through the West Gate and turning to right you soon reach a junction of three roads at Crossway Green: one of them goes north to split at the first village, St. Arvans, into two distinct routes for Monmouth; one—the Chepstow-Usk road—goes westward; the third road, between these two, passes Itton Court, an ancient but modernized Herbert mansion standing in a well-timbered park merging upwards into Chepstow Park Wood. At Crossway Green is the main entrance to Piercefield Park, the grounds of which, open once weekly, contain a series of belvederes—the "alcove," the "grotto," and so forth—sprinkled over the demesne by an eighteenth-century owner who thus so reduced his fortune that he ended his days as a Wye ferryman. It must be added that these excrescences disclose delightful vistas of the Wye and its farther bank. At Trelleck the three outstanding "curiosities"—are a group of monoliths, a tree-crowned motte,

[1] Yet after the battle of Banbury (1469) it was held for two years by Jasper Tudor.

127 THE TWIN SUMMITS OF THE BRECON BEACONS, SEEN FROM THE NORTH

128 THE HORSESHOE BEND OF THE WYE AT TIDENHAM,
NEAR CHEPSTOW

129 THE USK, BY LLANBADOCK BRIDGE, MONMOUTHSHIRE

and a mediæval "virtuous well"—and the arcades, windows and woodwork of its church, which also contains a childish drawing of the "curiosities" scratched on a sundial. Finally, the road descends in a breakneck zigzag, crosses the Trothy, skirts the Chippenham, Monmouth's spacious park, and passing through the old cappers' suburb[1] of Overmonnow, brings you over Monnow bridge and under the much-photographed bridge gateway (123) into the main street of Monmouth.

The other road from St. Arvans, the route which skirts the Wyndcliff and follows the winding Wye past Tintern Abbey, has been so frequently and exhaustively described that further description must be either superfluous or presumptuous. This Wye-bank road to Monmouth and its continuation to Ross form the nucleus of the "Wye Valley" trips organized by so many—too many—motor-charabanc companies. Though the scenery of this part of the Wye is superb and richly diversified, more sophisticated taste much prefers the tract between Builth and Boughrood or even the higher stretch between Llangurig and Newbridge-on-Wye, in which portions the river itself, clear and sparkling or foaming over rapids, is a most important factor of beauty.

Raglan, marking the end of the first stage of the pleasant Usk-Monmouth road, bears the characteristic signs of a trippers' Mecca, and æsthetically does not attract. Its famous castle (43), which to travellers from the south shows an extraordinarily long frontage, is exhaustively described in guidebooks obtainable locally. The "Yellow Tower of Gwent"—the detached hexagonal keep—and neighbouring gatehouse, the two spacious courts and the intervening hall and state apartment, are pleasant to look at and simple to comprehend.

Points that are noticeable along the Raglan-Monmouth route are the Elizabethan Dingestow Court, on a hillside to left; on the same side, perched conspicuously on a ridge-top across the Trothy, Wonastow church and Court; between Dingestow and Wonastow, a lonely row of cottages known as Single Street; on a hilltop opposite the latter, on your right, Craig-y-Dorth, where Glyndwr had his bandit lair after the Shrewsbury fiasco; and Mitchel Troy, a pleasant village with a pretty church. Other small, really picturesque churches close to Monmouth are Dixton, below the Ross road, and Rockfield, above the direct Abergavenny road.

The Honour of Monmouth was, after the de Montfort troubles, annexed to the Duchy of Lancaster and came later

[1] Fluellen's men wore Monmouth caps adorned with leeks.

into the hands of John of Gaunt; Henry V, his grandson, who in spite of Fluellen's typically Welsh flattery was not quite on a par with Alexander of Macedon, was born in Monmouth Castle, and his counterfeit presentment looks down from the façade of the eighteenth-century Shire Hall.

THE SCREEN BETTWS-Y-CRWYN CHURCH, CLUN FOREST
(Drawn by H. T. Timmins)

INDEX